Libra

The cryptocurrency revolution: How Facebook crypto will change the global banking system, detailed instructions on how to use it to make payments, investments, trading and differences from Bitcoin

[Robert Donegal]

Text Copyright © [Robert Donegal]

All rights reserved. No part of this guide may be reproduced in any form without permission in writing from the publisher except in the case of brief quotations embodied in critical articles or reviews.

Legal & Disclaimer

The information contained in this book and its contents is not designed to replace or take the place of any form of medical or professional advice; and is not meant to replace the need for independent medical, financial, legal or other professional advice or services, as may be required. The content and information in this book has been provided for educational and entertainment purposes only.

The content and information contained in this book has been compiled from sources deemed reliable, and it is accurate to the best of the Author's knowledge, information and belief. However, the Author cannot guarantee its accuracy and validity and cannot be held liable for any errors and/or omissions. Further, changes are periodically made to this book as and when needed. Where appropriate and/or necessary, you must consult a professional (including but not limited to your doctor, attorney, financial advisor or such other professional advisor) before using any of the suggested remedies, techniques, or information in this book.

Upon using the contents and information contained in this book, you agree to hold harmless the Author from and against any damages, costs, and expenses, including any legal fees potentially resulting from the application of any of the information provided by this book. This disclaimer applies to any loss, damages or injury caused by the use and application, whether directly or indirectly, of any advice or information presented, whether for breach of contract, tort, negligence, personal injury, criminal intent, or under any other cause of action.

You agree to accept all risks of using the information presented inside this book.

You agree that by continuing to read this book, where appropriate and/or necessary, you shall consult a professional (including but not limited to your doctor, attorney, or financial advisor or such other advisor as needed) before using any of the suggested remedies, techniques, or information in this book.

Table of Contents

Introduction 1

Chapter 1: What is Libra 5

   Main benefits & disadvantages 7

Chapter 2: Differences from Bitcoins and other Crypto currencies 8

   Basic Principles of Cryptocurrency and the Batman of Our Times 10

      The Advantages of Cryptocurrency 13

      The Inventor of Bitcoin And Why He's the Batman of Our Times 15

   Bitcoin Mastery 18

   Finding Your Own Bitcoin 23

   How the Blockchain Technology Is Changing the Future of Money, Economy, and Our World 29

Chapter 3: How different is Bitcoin from regular currency? 38

   Bitcoin in business 45

   many banks are approaching Libra cautiously, citing regulatory uncertainty. Regulations around How to Store Bitcoins and Other Cryptocurrencies 51

Chapter 3: Possible future development of Libra in the world 58

Retail 58

Trading 58

Financial systems 59

Know Your Customer (KYC) implications 59

    What is a smart contract? 60

The Internet of Things 66

Different Blockchains 67

    Blockchain vs Hashgraph 68

    Blockchain vs Tangle 71

Chapter 4: The Libra and Block chain 74

Most popular cryptocurrencies and why they matter? 74

Blockchain Potential in the Non-Financial Sector 76

Implications for the Future of Blockchain Technology 85

Implications of Blockchain: Big Data, Privacy, and Personal Data 89

    Profiting from Blockchain Technologies 94

    Limitations & Challenges of Blockchain Technology 102

    Speed 102

    Scaling 103

    Quantum computing 105

Chapter 5: The reasons why Libra will be a success. 107

Chapter 6: Why Facebook will be the new global bank 111

Chapter 7: How to pay with Libra............................ 114

Chapter 8: Methods on how to invest with Libra 118

Chapter 9: Some key points about Libra 124

Chapter 10: What the Libra skeptics think 133

Chapter 11: Frequently asked questions about Libra 137

Conclusions... 141

Introduction

Finally, after two long years of speculation, Facebook founder Mark Zuckerberg has revealed to the world his latest brilliant idea, so insane as to have alerted analysts around the world.

From 2020 Libra will be a new cryptocurrency available to make purchases and to transfer money online.

The announcement in itself did not come without some shock.

In fact, for some time now there had been numerous rumours about the entry of Facebook, the giant of Menlo Park, into the world of cryptocurrency.

Sentences that, after careful analysis, go far beyond a simple slogan for presentation and that reveal most of Libra's strengths.

Despite everything, there are already many who are ready to bet on this new cryptocurrency; the reasons are many and we will analyze them one by one.

But should we only consider Libra as a new crypto currency or should we frame it in a wider economic system?

To understand how big this revolution will be, it is enough to change your point of view and observe Libra through the eyes of ordinary people, of those who today (the vast majority of the population) have at most heard of Bitcoin but who know absolutely nothing about cryptocurrencies and the technology that is at their base.

This time the battle between Bitcoin and Libra will not take place on the ground of calculations, technology or on that of profits or even privacy and security.

Today, we are talking about a revolutionary new digital currency that, for the first time, will involve billions of users around the world, different from each other especially in habits and education.

Libra has the potential to aspire to become a global cryptocurrency, and most likely for a long time, the only global cryptocurrency.

Much more is at stake, even the very survival of most cryptocurrencies currently in circulation.

Also Bitcoin, the king of cryptocurrencies, will undergo a very important downturn.

But there will also be repercussions to traditional currencies as the whole system of making purchases and business will be affected by this novelty.

Think for a moment.

If Libra's destiny were to be to retrace the success of Facebook, what would be the right moves to make today?

What would be the possible evolution of Libra?

Facebook was born, almost for fun in 2003, in one of the most famous universities in the United States, created by some anonymous students, among who today stands out the name of a man known throughout the world: Mark Zuckerberg.

Surrounded only by the university area and under the name of Facemash, the idea that came to life has revolutionized in a few years the lives and habits of all the inhabitants of this planet.

Do you remember Netlog, My Space or Windows Live Messenger?

Many of those who were considered giants were swept away in an instant by a revolutionary project and about which few had understood from the beginning its real potential.

If today you could access a time machine and return to 2004, who wouldn't bet "all in" on Facebook?

The situation that currently flows before our eyes is probably the same as sixteen years ago.

We have again a visionary idea that makes its way into a territory that already has its giants (Bitcoin, Ethereum, Litecoin etc. ...).

The question to ask is therefore only one: where will Libra exist?

The only thing certain is that whoever first takes the right wave, will find himself first on the crest, ready to ride it towards a rosy future.

In these pages we go to analyze the five salient points that will be decisive for the success of this new and revolutionary cryptocurrency.

Chapter 1: What is Libra

Libra is actually an effort to sell current payment facilities by reinventing and enhancing bitcoin ten years after its launch. While it may take minutes to verify Bitcoin transactions and may cost several USD, Libra should move for negligible charges within seconds. While the cost of Bitcoin is highly volatile, the swings of Libra should be minimal as it is supported by a currency basket. And while a bitcoin transaction requires more than 1,000 kWh of computing power, Libra transactions should consume no more energy than credit card transactions.

Libra is created by buying coins with USD, ultimately exchanging first digital currency. These cash inflows form the reserve that is going to support the currency. Local regulators can hold tabs on Libra, which is not going to generate interest. The "wallet" suppliers, that enable customers to send and receive the currency, will be required to comply with domestic regulations, such as those against money laundering.

The company will decentralize decision-making on Libra to assist those concerned about allowing Facebook into their economic affairs. Its institutional core is an organization consisting of a wide spectrum of economic parties, including financial firms and non-profit groups. Their main task is to monitor the blockchain, a database that tracks who owns the

Libra coin. This organization should have 100 participants on the release of the currency, each of whom can run one of the blockchain nodes.

The currency will be provided to 2.4bn Facebook users, although in order to Libra to work efficiently, many companies will need to accept it. "Incentive programs" will be run by the association, mainly subsidies to get individuals to use and keep the new currency. Subsidies will be raised from membership fees that all of 100 participating parties will need to deposit: $10 m each for a total of $1bn. Facebook is not going to be the only wallet supplier.

However, the association will have to guarantee that Calibra, the distinct subsidiary established by Facebook to offer payments from Libra, does not have an unfair benefit over other companies. While WeChat and Alibaba, two Chinese Internet giants, did in China, Facebook itself is likely to create a suite of financial services.

Main benefits & disadvantages

Benefits:

- stable price unlike other cryptocurrencies;
- Libra coins will be convertible back to fiat currency in banks or other financial institutions;
- Quick payments, easy to buy;
- huge platform with over 2 billion customers;
- global currency which can be used to exchange for any currency;
- buy goods, rent a car, do the shopping, pay for your restaurant bills, etc. with just one simple click and no transaction fees.

Disadvantages:

- for crypto investors, there is no point to invest for price speculation;
- anyone can develop a similar app and can barge into your account;
- criminals can snatch your personal information and can steal your currency;
- great risk of your data and FB profile being stolen;

Chapter 2: Differences from Bitcoins and other Crypto currencies

Before breaking new ground, real professionals learn the rules of the game and set goals, determining what kind of result they want to achieve. Since we are professionals, we will first deal with this task.

Having set the goals, it is important to understand what is needed for a successful and fast startup in the cryptocurrency market. You will be surprised, but the theory is the least important thing in this field. Many people say they lack the information and knowledge for doing this type of business. However, most of the strategies I will tell you about do not require deep knowledge of the cryptocurrency business world. It will be enough for you to have a grip on basic principles of the cryptocurrency economy.

Then what's the problem? You need practice. Only practice, not a book (not even mine), will help you to understand where to buy, where to sell, how to store, and how to transfer cryptocurrency.

You will also need:

- Several ready-made strategies with low risk to enter the market

- Ability to filter content and information around you
- Communication with more experienced traders of the cryptocurrency market and "spying" on their actions
- Risk management
- An audit from an experienced curator.

And now we proceed to the statement you must remember once and for all: making any investment in the cryptocurrency market IS A RISK. If you are not ready to accept this, don't bother trying. Any opinion or forecast for the development of a particular coin, the reliability of ICO (this will be discussed later) is only a biased stance. There is not a single person across the globe who could give you an iron-clad guarantee for further developments. There are absolutely no right decisions and 100% guarantees. I or someone else can only give you a piece of advice, not guarantees.

The cryptocurrency market is alive and constantly changing. Therefore, when dealing with cryptocurrency trading, one must learn to take personal responsibility for making decisions and always remember that no gains can be made without taking risks. Yes, there are less risky strategies, but risks exist in any case. Invest just the sum you are willing to lose without much regret.

And right now, lay the book aside and write down the two rules you should never break:

1. Do not invest to the last penny.
2. Have a stash of cash to take advantage of opportunities.

And finally, beginners should learn several safety points:

- When trading on the exchange, protect your account with two-factor authentication and keep your code name private.
- Your password should have at least 26 characters; a special password generator may help you come up with one.
- Never keep all your money on one exchange or in one wallet.
- Trade only on tried-and-true exchanges.
- Do not use public access points to trade in the cryptocurrency market.

Basic Principles of Cryptocurrency and the Batman of Our Times

Let's take a roundabout approach to this topic, starting from the banking sector.

The entire banking system of our days, regardless of the country, is arranged in such a way that we do not own our money. Central banks in any state hold emission monopoly, which is provided through legislation, creating a sure stumbling block to cryptocurrency legalization.

Fiat money is a term used by the cryptocurrency community to designate a currency without intrinsic value as money by government regulation or law (dollar, euro, etc.).

In theory, this currency should be secured by at least those goods, products, or services that are produced in the territory of a particular country (GDP) so that every citizen of this country can change their personal money for products. All the banks of the country also undertake the same currency, and the central bank promises to maintain its stability and reliability. This is how it works in theory, but no one can actually guarantee the currency's stability.

The government of a country is the main customer of all goods and services for the population, i.e. one of the largest employers. It is also the largest customer for the construction of roads, houses, hospitals, schools, etc. This makes up the lion's share of the GDP of each particular country. Accordingly, the government ensures the life of the population – pays pensions and social benefits. All these funds are taken from the central bank, which can issue currency and finance the government.

A policy dubbed **quantitative easing** was once implemented in the USA and later even spread to Europe and Japan. Due to this phenomenon, the amount of money in the world has greatly increased, while the purchasing power of the dollar has decreased over the past 100 years by 95%. This trend is ongoing. The more money exists, the cheaper it becomes.

It is important to keep in mind that each kind of currency experiences inflation, which indicates the depreciation of currency over some time. In other words, inflation is the speed of money circulation. The country's economy has its own cycles as people take on loans and then pay them back.

I cannot help but mention these loans. In the USA, the loan interest rates are at an average of 1%. They remained at zero level for a long time in the past. The central banks issued money and bought up financial assets, and accordingly, the poor people remained poor, and those people who had financial assets, stocks, or real estate made a constant profit. That is why each crisis makes the poor even poorer and the rich even richer. These processes result in a very powerful stratification of the population. However, alas, the economy works in this way, and we approach a kind of dead end, as many financial analysts state. All of this to demonstrate that the central banks do not cope very well with their function.

So people started to look for an alternative way to preserve the value of money. If not to multiply, at least not to lose. That's why many people invest in gold, fixed income instruments, shares, etc. At the same time, the economy began to develop swiftly after the Internet appeared, so people realized they do not need to hold money in physical form now. Thus, the concept of electronic money emerged.

The idea of creating a digital currency like Bitcoin is not entirely new. Still, there is a difference between Bitcoin and other types of digital money. If you use such electronic money systems as PayPal, Western Union, or Skrill, your finances are stored in the same companies. In this case, we deal with centralized money management, i.e. the fate of your money depends on decisions of specific people in these companies. You have no power to influence these decisions.

The Advantages of Cryptocurrency

Cryptocurrency is quite a different thing. This decentralized currency is characterized by the independence from a single transaction processing center. It is very difficult to track cryptocurrency transactions and impossible to cancel them. Using this type of currency, two people can carry out a purchase and sale transaction directly on the Internet, without resorting to the center of financial transactions.

But let's discuss in more detail the advantages of cryptocurrency over fiat money. These advantages are obvious!

☐ Emission and circulation standards: **cryptocurrency is established once, and it is inviolable, while the standards for fiat money are changed arbitrarily by the central banks.**

☐ The issue **is carried out: cryptocurrency flows from the network to the participant while fiat money flows from the central bank to banks, from banks to companies, and only from companies to participants.**

☐ The flow of funds: **direct for cryptocurrency; through banks, payment systems, and cash for fiat money.**

☐ The number of participants: **5 million for cryptocurrency; 7 billion for fiat money.**

☐ Transaction speed: **high for cryptocurrency; low for fiat money.**

☐ Anonymity: **always possible for cryptocurrency; sometimes possible when dealing with cash for fiat money.**

☐ Inflation: **impossible only for cryptocurrency; a constant reality for fiat money.**

- **Rate volatility**: definitely high for cryptocurrency; low for fiat money.

The Inventor of Bitcoin And Why He's the Batman of Our Times

In the midst of the global financial crisis of 2008, somebody under the name of Satoshi Nakamoto designed Bitcoin and created its original reference implementation. Bitcoin became a new type of digital currency, which was very different from all the others. Its main difference lies in the fact that it is decentralized. Therefore, each participant cannot influence its fate.

Bitcoin is, perhaps, the final frontier when it comes to currency in different areas around the world. It is a method of payment that does not discriminate between countries, rich, poor or anything else that could identify a person. Bitcoin was created to be able to trade money terms without ever having to use money and it is a perfect solution for the need to have something other than a typical bank for currency options. Those who use Bitcoin can understand how freeing it is to be able to rely on themselves instead of having to use the currency options that most banks have available for them.

Use

The availability of Bitcoin in major retail locations is something that is relatively new. Many people do not even know what Bitcoin is so it is somewhat hard for retailers to offer that as an option for the people who want to be able to use it.

Because it has become increasingly popular due to the fact that it is worth much more than what it once was, it has recently been featured at major retailers, like Overstock, a company that specializes in online sales and helps people who want to be able to purchase the majority of their necessities online.

The single biggest use of Bitcoin is from person to person. Second is from business to business and person to business or business to person comes in as the last spot for uses of Bitcoin in the sense of entity to entity.

Safety

Because of the way that Bitcoin is set up, it is much safer for people to use Bitcoin and other forms of cryptocurrency than it is for them to use traditional cash or even credit cards. Bitcoin is a type of currency that is exclusively online. Unless your wallet gets hacked by someone who wants to get your currency, there is virtually no way to have it stolen. Even if it does get hacked, it is encrypted so that it can be traced exactly back to the wallet that holds the Bitcoin that was stolen from you out of your own wallet.

Physical Attributes

There are, essentially, no physical attributes of Bitcoin. This is because the currency is exclusively online and it is more of an idea or a series of codes than anything else. Unlike cash or credit cards, you are not able to put the Bitcoin in your wallet and you cannot actually ever hold the currency in your hand.

This can be seen as both a good and bad thing – it is nearly impossible to lose it or steal it but you also are at the mercy of the computer system and the host that holds all of the codes for Bitcoin. What happens if it crashes?

Trades Between Countries

With more people getting involved in Bitcoin, it is easy for them to recognize that they are going to be able to use it for many different types of transactions. In the past, businesses or individuals who were in different countries had to wire money from person to person. It was complicated and the exchange rate got in the way of being able to get the exact amount to the other party. Now, with Bitcoin, everyone who uses it around the world uses the same form of currency. There is no need for exchange rates, bank transfers or even a wait time that is sometimes needed with money that is wired.

Anonymous Users

Perhaps one of the most popular aspects of Bitcoin, especially by those who used it in the early days, is the anonymity that comes with Bitcoin. While your name is technically attached to a wallet number, it is difficult to show your identity when you are using Bitcoin. If you want to be able to keep your identity secure and private, you will be able to do so with Bitcoin because of the different aspects that are included with your wallet. You're identified by a username or a wallet ID instead of being identified by your own name as you would be at a bank.

Bitcoin Mastery

The idea behind Bitcoin is that it makes life easier for those who enjoy the Internet and technology. It is something that is helpful for many people but only if they know the right way to use it.

Anyone can go out and purchase Bitcoin but to really get the best use of Bitcoin and make money from it, you will need to make sure that you know the basics of it.

It does not take much to become a Bitcoin master and the following steps will teach you exactly what you need to make sure that you are going to be able to become the best that you can be when you are dealing with Bitcoin.

Purchase of Bitcoin

The single most popular option for purchasing Bitcoin is to buy it from a site or app like Coin Base. This is a company that deals only in Bitcoin and they rule the market so that people can make sure that they are getting the best experience possible with Bitcoin. It is something that they have worked hard to build up and something that most people who use Bitcoin trust to be able to buy their Bitcoin from.

When you buy your Bitcoin from Coin Base, you will have many different options to choose from. You can simply use your credit or debit card to buy the Bitcoin or you can choose to use a bank account. With a bank account, as long as Coin Base can verify it, you will be able to buy a much larger amount of Bitcoin at one time because of the parameters that are set up with Bank accounts.

It is a good idea to try and make sure that you know where you are going to buy from. While Coin Base is the most popular option for people to buy Bitcoin from, you can also choose other sites to purchase from. Before the Silk Road was shut down by the FBI, there were hundreds of places to buy Bitcoin – now, there is only a handful.

Coin Base seems to be the best option for those who are just getting started with Bitcoin because you can buy, trade and even sell your Bitcoin right from the app.

Getting Rid of Bitcoin

At some point, you will probably want to offload some of the Bitcoin that you have. Most people do this from an investment perspective and you should only do it when you know that you are going to be able to profit from it. This is an important factor of Bitcoin and something that you will need to keep in mind before you sell it off.

The one way that you can get rid of your Bitcoin is to use it for purchases but that will cause you to not get the most value out of your Bitcoin.

Selling it is the best way to get a return on your Bitcoin investment and it is something that you need to do if you want to make money. You can sell right through Coin Base so that you can get the amount returned on the investment that you have made. Another way that you can make money from Bitcoin is simply selling to another individual. You may not get as much as what you would like for it but you will not have to worry about the fees that come with selling on Coin Base.

Where You Can Use Bitcoin

There are a few places online that you can use Bitcoin. These places are increasing and even some big name brand companies have started to use Bitcoin as a form of currency. Places like Overstock.com and even Facebook allow you to pay for goods and services on them. This is something that is much different from what was allowed in previous years.

If you are hoping to use your Bitcoin for **everything** that you purchase online, you can use one of the many Bitcoin marketplaces. These are set up in a similar fashion to an online store but you can use your Bitcoin to buy everything from a new house to a hover board to even services that you can use in real life. The biggest differences in these Bitcoin marketplaces is that the only form of currency accepted at each of them is Bitcoin. You can't just use your credit card to pay and you must have a Bitcoin wallet number to even be able to enter the marketplace where you purchase these items.

Investment of Bitcoin

Most people who choose to use Bitcoin are actually doing so as an investment. They don't do it so that they can buy things online and they certainly don't do it to join the marketplaces but they, instead, do it so that they can make the most out of the money that they have invested in it. Similar to other types of trades, people who invest in Bitcoin are actually able to sell it off for a profit later on. The people who initially invested in Bitcoin are actually making huge profits because of the change in the price of Bitcoin.

Changes in Price

As the market has changed and Bitcoin has become increasingly popular, the price has skyrocketed. What was originally not worth much is now worth a large amount. In fact, Bitcoin is one of the fastest (and largest per margin) growing investments that have made their way onto the market in the past 20 years. It is something that has been able to grow from a very small amount of money to a much larger amount and people are learning that they stand to make a lot of money from the investments.

The change in price all depends on the popularity of the investment. The more popular something is, the more it increases in price. Bitcoin is no different. As the demand for it rises, the price increases. There is no shortage of supply of Bitcoin but it is something that is going to continue to rise because of the huge demand that is out there for it. Just 10 years ago, nobody had ever heard of Bitcoin. Now, about 50% of people have heard about it and even more want in on the action. With a market that is nearly impossible to saturate, Bitcoin is expected to increase in price for years to come.

Organically Finding Bitcoin

You don't have to just rely on buying Bitcoin. Some of the biggest Bitcoin owners in the world have actually found their own Bitcoin without paying any money for it. This is through the process of mining. While you will learn a lot more about mining in the next chapter, it is important for you to know that buying it isn't the only way to get it and those who choose to mine Bitcoin are actually able to make decent profits off of the Bitcoin that they have found all on their own.

Your Wallet

The wallet that you have for your Bitcoin is something that is very important. This is where you hold the Bitcoin but it is also where all of your transactions will happen. In the world of Bitcoin, you are nothing more than a wallet. This is because you need your wallet ID to make trades, buy Bitcoin and even sell it off for a profit. If you want to purchase anything, at all, with Bitcoin, you need to have a wallet along with a wallet ID that will tie you to the Bitcoin that you have built up in that same wallet.

Finding Your Own Bitcoin

There are many different ways to mine for Bitcoin and some people have found that other methods work better than what works for other people. While mining Bitcoin can be very profitable, it is something that you should only attempt if you have the technological and mathematical know-how along with the ability to spend a lot of time looking for it.

With Bitcoin mining, it is possible to make a lot of money but you must invest a lot of time. For example, some people will spend up to an entire week just to be able to find a single Bitcoin.

Community Aspect

For Bitcoin to be able to work, there need to be certain mathematical problems that are solved. These are all created through the use of algorithms and they make the money encrypted. If miners are able to do this, they can find the code for the Bitcoin.

The community made it so that anyone would be able to mine for it. This allows the codes to get solved but it also gives people the motivation that they need to be able to find their own Bitcoin. Even those who are broke can start investing in Bitcoin but they have to have the know-how.

The Basics

When someone wants to be able to mine Bitcoin, they simply have to go into the database and do many searches for the problems that need to be solved. These are complicated and they may end up solving and sifting through hundreds of them before they find one that will turn into a Bitcoin code. It is something that, if done manually, would take thousands upon thousands of hours to even find one. When Bitcoin first started, it was much simpler.

After people learned about mining, they decided to start creating machines that would give them the chance to be able to mine for the Bitcoin that they wanted. This was all computer work and often involved building their own systems so that they could create the perfect mining machines. It is something that people still do and the majority of miners have systems that they have created for the sole purpose of finding Bitcoin. They have entire computers and network systems that are dedicated to being able to mine Bitcoin.

The machines are often built from scratch and involve the use of the Raspberry Pi systems which allow people to build their own programs.

As a Miner

The majority of miners who try to find Bitcoin started out as a hobby. After they found their first Bitcoin, they were able to then build from there with the money that they made. It was something that gave them the motivation that they needed to be able to find Bitcoin. Some people have such in depth systems that are so good at finding Bitcoin that they are Bitcoin miners on a full-time basis and that is how they make their money. They then are able to invest their earnings because Bitcoin is something that is always going up in value.

Many of the miners who are now finding large numbers of Bitcoin on a regular basis are ones who originally started out with mining. Around 50% of the people who are now mining for Bitcoin were among the first people who were mining Bitcoin.

They have learned how to find the best math problems, create the algorithms and get the most amount of money from the Bitcoin that they have found.

Help from Bitcoin

While there is no way for Bitcoin to actually help the miners out with the searches that they are doing, it is something that people can find benefits from. The more Bitcoin that they have, the more that they can benefit from the different computer systems that they are able to afford to build when they are doing different things.

Having a lot of money in Bitcoin does not necessarily make it easier for people to find more Bitcoin but it does give them the chance to be able to make more complicated and in depth machines. When they are able to have the most sophisticated machine, they will also be able to get the most Bitcoin from using the machine to mine.

The creators of Bitcoin have very little to do with the cryptocurrency now. Even if they were heavily involved, they would not know all of the answers to the mathematical problems. That is because they designed Bitcoin in a way that allows them to give everyone equal chances to be able to find the money. As long as someone has the skill to build the machine and the know how to solve the problems that are included with most Bitcoin mining opportunities, they can invest in Bitcoin and make money from that investment.

Bitcoin is truly an equal opportunity.

You Need Hardware

There is almost no way to mine for Bitcoin without hardware with all of the people who are currently mining for it. In the past, people were able to mine it manually, solve the problems and even find it in different areas. That is not the case anymore and it is something that can be really detrimental for those who do not have the hardware to be able to find it. There is no way to make a sustainable income through the use of Bitcoin mining.

The good news, though, is that if you have one Bitcoin or even if you have somehow managed to spend an outrageous amount of time looking for a single Bitcoin, you do have the money to create your own machine. In general, getting a Raspberry Pi system and setting it up to be able to use should only cost you a couple hundred dollars – far less than the 2017 price of Bitcoin.

Finding one Bitcoin or purchasing one can then lead to you having the financial ability to be able to set up your own mining machine and finding a lot of Bitcoin that you can then make money from.

Starting Out

Most people who start out will have computer-based knowledge. They will know how to set up hardware and they will have an idea of what it takes to be able to get the different aspects of mining done for Bitcoin.

If you are going to mine the Bitcoin, it is worth looking at different options. There are many sites where you can practice the mining process and these sites will give you a good idea of what you will be able to do with the Bitcoin that you have or that you are going to be looking for.

Always make sure that you are really ready to start mining Bitcoin. It is not only an investment that you will need to make with the money that you have but it is also a huge time investment. You should be prepared to spend a lot of time looking for Bitcoin and trying to build the machines that will help you to find Bitcoin. No matter where you are or what you do with Bitcoin, you cannot just jump right into mining.

Learn as much as you can about Bitcoin mining and then try your hand at it to avoid wasted time and money.

How the Blockchain Technology Is Changing the Future of Money, Economy, and Our World

A blockchain is a decentralized or distributed ledger that stores records of digital transactions. Contrary to the working modalities of a bank, government, or accountants who use a centralized database, a blockchain/distributed ledger has replicated and distributed via the internet databases that are visible for all within the network to see (this ties in with what we discussed in section 2). A blockchain can be public, as is the case with Bitcoins, or they can be private like an intranet.

Since the blockchain is decentralized, open to the scrutiny of all within the network, and at the same time cryptic, it has all the characteristics of a disruptive technology that promise to change how we view and transact with money, how economies around the world operate, and even how the world operates when it comes to transactions.

Here is how Bitcoins and the blockchain technology are going to change the world:

1: Programmable money

Have you ever given your child money and worried that he or she would use the money to buy something other than the original intent—perhaps you give your teenage son money for lunch but instead, he buys pot? If you have, you don't have to worry about that anymore.

Bitcoins, and in extension, most monies using the blockchain technology, are programmable money meaning you can program the purpose of the money and even things such as in which city or country the money is used. You can program the currency to a specific use, perhaps buying textbooks, and reject all other uses. While this is not very common, the blockchain protocol allows it and in the future, you may see further exploitation of this.

2: Faster and Cheaper Money Transfer

The blockchain is the first decentralized form of currency. Today, the technology has become so popular that banks and money transfer services are looking for ways through which they can exploit these technologies.

Mainstream adaptation of blockchain technology and the transference of cryptocurrencies around the world will disrupt services such as Western Union and because the blockchain technology offers faster, secure, and minimal transaction charges, this technology is poised for a very disruptive takeoff that will shift how we send money to each other and how economies function.

3: A Flourishing Business Environment

Various governmental institutions around the world are acknowledging Bitcoins for what they are, new business opportunities that when well tapped and given governmental support, would translate into jobs and industrial growth. Increased adaptation of this technology, which with the internet of things, is where we are headed, will lead to bullish economic growth all round.

4: Intrinsic Value Appreciation

With inflation being on the increase in almost all parts of the world, banking fiat currencies in bank in the hopes that you will draw interest is a foolhardy venture. The innate design of cryptocurrencies is that with time, their value appreciates and as Bitcoins near their 21 million cap, you can bet that their value shall soar unperturbed by inflation.

Think of it this way, if you had bought 1 BTC worth $15 in 2012, today, that same BTC (Bitcoin) would be worth $1000. Do you think the same value would apply to the same amount banked?

In truth, application of the blockchain technology is largely in cryptocurrencies. In the future, you will see this technology used on things such as smart contract, the management of patient health records, electronic voting, etc.

This technology is poised to, like Uber or Airbnb, disrupt banking and financial institutions, insurance, health care, academia, the public sector and all other sectors of the economy that rely on intermediaries. As you can guess, this disruption shall cause immense transformation and with it, the loss of jobs.

While this may be so, like Ford's assembly line, the disruption shall bring with it positive benefits too.

For example, after the removal of the impediment banks place on the free flow of currency by charging exuberant fees and inane regulatory requirements—in some jurisdictions, you cannot send a specific amount of money—we shall witness a fluid flow of cash around the globe, which will lead to improved global trade.

The blockchain will foster better, quicker, and frequent trade between people (because of the safety of it and the low transaction charges), something that promises to decentralize, democratize, and expand global financial systems thus offering people better payment systems and stronger protection against frauds and exploitation.

At first, hailed as a defiant innovation that would overturn the world's money related foundations and free individuals from the burdensome charges and controls of the financial foundation, the digital currency has since been discolored by crime and wild market theory. And keeping in mind that everybody has known about crypto names like Bitcoin, not many individuals comprehend the basics of how digital forms of money really work — particularly with regards to the individual fund. This is what you have to know to keep you from getting ripped off, and furthermore help you decide whether digital forms of money are for you.

Cryptographic money is fundamentally an advanced method to hold and move esteem on the web. You can buy digital money tokens or coins on the web (with a Visa or "customary" cash), and there is ordinarily nobody individual or bank that controls specific cryptographic money.

The estimation of any digital money at some random time relies upon free market activity. There's generally a fixed measure of any cash accessible at some random minute, so the more individuals need to utilize it, the higher the cost. In late 2017, for instance, the cost of a solitary Bitcoin took off to generally $20,000 and after that took a drive to around $4,000.

On the off chance that you have your very own wallet under your very own advanced lock and key, you can "send" individuals computerized reserves. To do this, the vast majority will in general utilize online vaults, similar to those given by Coinbase. The procedure is fundamentally the same as conventional online administrations: you essentially enter the measure of cash you need to send and the organization you need to pay.

A few sellers acknowledge digital currencies. Microsoft will give you a chance to add Bitcoin to your record web based utilizing your computerized wallet, for instance. What's more, there's a developing rundown of things you can buy with digital currency, including everything from compelling artwork to land. By and large, the reception of digital money installments has been to a greater extent an advertising move than a down to earth budgetary one, however it can give cryptographic money tokens greater steadiness.

On the drawback, you ought to know that a large portion of the outlets that acknowledge digital money additionally put huge confinements and impediments on it. In any case, most just acknowledge the main cryptographic forms of money, Bitcoin and Ethereum. Second, you will most likely be unable to utilize the credit for each administration. For instance, Microsoft will give you a chance to utilize Bitcoin to purchase diversions, films, and applications in Windows and Xbox stores — yet you can't utilize it in the Microsoft online store or purchase gift vouchers with it.

There is a large portion of the autonomous and startup trades that will purchase and sell cryptographic forms of money for you additionally charge a type of expense for the administration. What's more, similar to genuine stock representatives, they make you come and go, at whatever point you purchase or sell cash.

That relies upon your point of view. The facts demonstrate that cryptographic forms of money that utilization blockchain innovation guarantee that exchanges are recorded appropriately and make it hard to hack. Blockchain programming is a decentralized record that no single individual or organization controls because the record of all exchanges are kept up over different hubs, offering excess and making it amazingly hard for any one client to mess with.

Notwithstanding, if a cryptographic money token is stolen from an advanced wallet, much of the time that implies the cash is away for good and untraceable. Besides, a few vaults have been hacked as much as of a few million dollars, again leaving clients with no response because the assets are not insured or guaranteed by any administration establishment (balance this with conventional ledgers in the US, which the FDIC conceals for to $200,000). A year ago, over $1 billion was stolen from cryptographic money trades.

Generally, crypto was the domain of hoodlums and advanced theorists who were likely pulled in by the simplicity with which Bitcoin can be exchanged online without trading off namelessness. Individuals who traffic in stolen information and medications on the dull web were enormous starting advocates of digital currency. In any case, it has picked up authenticity in the course of recent years as a result of its adaptability for moving computerized cash online without the requirement for any type of institutional banking. It has likewise picked up support in nations like Venezuela where the nearby cash is insecure and subject to wild inflationary swings. In these circumstances, the digital currency can offer some security against political agitation.

In a word, no. The crucial issue with all digital forms of money is the eccentric change in their worth. So while you clutch a specific computerized section, you could be losing (or picking up) cash until you use it to purchase something or empty it. Conventional cash (what crypto advocates allude to as "fiat" money) will, in general, be progressively steady since it's upheld by governments and a lot bigger system of worldwide exchanging markets.

Indeed and no. The theoretical air pocket of 2017 on the planet's most prominent digital money, Bitcoin, burst — yet Bitcoin is still broadly utilized. Individuals work together in Bitcoin in what might be compared to up to $800 million every day. That may sound like a great deal, however, it's not exactly 50% of what one customary administration, Paypal, does every day.

Be that as it may, it is picking up acknowledgment as a class of cash, to a great extent since privately owned businesses see huge promoting potential — and another wellspring of income — in propelling their cryptographic forms of money (see ICOs beneath).

For the most part, you can just utilize the tokens you purchase to buy administrations or items from that organization. So ICOs are useless anyplace else and there is dependably the threat that the organization will neglect to create anything worth purchasing — and there's no real way to recover your cash.

Besides, ICOs have been issued in a few tricks, leaving purchasers between a rock and a hard place. Also, there's an impressive theoretical market too, with some auxiliary markets jumping up and dealers trading the tokens on the web and driving up their worth.

A turn off the idea from ICOs is for privately owned businesses to issue their cryptographic money to be utilized distinctly at its stores. It can likewise be utilized like extra miles or focuses, redeemable later on for the organization's administrations. One major player taking a shot at its digital money for online cash trades is Facebook. Be that as it may, its prosperity — like that of a wide range of cryptographic money — will rely upon how much individuals trust it.

Chapter 3: How different is Bitcoin from regular currency?

Currently there are about 180 currencies that are being circulated and used around the world, at least the ones that are legally recognized by the United Nations. Although many historians and scholars would argue that the first instance of humans using a formal form of money dates as far back as a thousand decades (or more) ago, way back before human prehistory, in record and in the books, the British pound holds the record for being the world's oldest currency that is still being used today. The British pound was recorded to be used as early as the 8th century and until today the British continue to make use of this currency.

But what is money exactly? It appears that it's nothing more bit a token or symbol that societies developed to perform uninformed and more efficient trade. Barter system has been around within human communities as early as the 10th millennium BC, and it was almost inevitable for humans to develop a form of recognized trade. So now instead of having to exchange live cattle or bags of grain for a yard full of scarf, we get to enjoy the benefits and convenience that current currency affords us.

In its simplest core, Bitcoin could also serve as money as it also fulfills the simplest technical attributes of money. First, bitcoin is durable in a sense that it provides stability and that long-lasting property common money have. Like money we use now, we can do all sorts of math with bitcoin as well, we can add it up, subtract from it, divide it and even multiply its value. Bitcoin is mutually interchangeable in that you can barter and purchase goods with it. Bitcoin is easily transferable, in fact one of the advantages and appeals of bitcoin is its mobility and ease of transport and use. And finally, and possibly what most central banks are putting much effort in maintaining their currencies into, bitcoin is almost impossible to counterfeit.

However, there has still been a lot of heated debate whether bitcoin should be considered a currency or not. Faultfinders might criticize that bitcoin does not seem to fulfill the main functions of conventional money. First off, it is not even tangible! But supporters of the Bitcoin technology would heavily argue that an asset does not have to be tangible to be valuable.

In this chapter, we shall talk about the properties of bitcoin that reflects its role in economics and how it may, or may not be, like conventional currency.

1. Medium of exchange

As of date, tens of thousands are now patronizing bitcoin and are using it to conduct their businesses. With this information, there appears to be an obvious practical data that would support the idea that bitcoin can serve as a medium of exchange. Since its introduction into society, there seems to be a steady increase in the number of transactions utilizing bitcoin in their business. There are close to a hundred thousand transactions in the Bitcoin network per day, and although this is still considerably lower than other conventional currencies it has been used as a medium of exchange.

Traditional economists may say that for it to be recognized as a universal medium of exchange, the number of users must continue to expand and increase. But it appears that Bitcoin only needs to continue improving and expanding its network and it'll only be a few years until it can finally reach its critical mass point, or that instance where the benefits to the inexperienced users will exceed the cost of having to adapt to the innovative technology. In other words, to be considered a universal medium of exchange, Bitcoin should be used by at least a steady number of users so that for performing transactions, users wouldn't have to resort to other currencies because bitcoin affords them the convenience and efficiency.

2. Bitcoin's volatility

Possibly the biggest concern critics and supporters alike would have of Bitcoin technology is its volatility or its liability to change rapidly and unpredictably. Since 2011, Bitcoin's value has spiked up to 1200 its initial value by the start of 2014 only to dip a sharp decrease a couple months after, and today it plays around the 1000 value mark, the value continues to be very volatile. With this property, it is not surprising for economists and investors and money enthusiasts to consider the technology as a highly risky investment than as a stable store of value.

This unpredictable nature of bitcoin is often likened to the dynamics of a start-up business. Bitcoin is indeed increasing in value, however its speed of being utilized as a primary medium of exchange is not as competitive as conventional currencies or digital currencies for that matter. This low turnover of Bitcoin is because a lot of users who are diving into the Bitcoin network are holding on to their bitcoins as an investment instead of using it in circulation as a medium of exchange. In fact, Bitcoin has been associated with such high values that most bitcoins are now being held and kept under stagnant accounts. This phenomenon has been termed the **hoarding** of bitcoins.

A currency's property to function as a medium of exchange and as an item to be used with higher purchasing value in the future are complementary properties. No one would resort to the currency if they do not have value, on the one hand if they had too much value no one would want to keep using and circulating them for fear of missing out on probable future investments. The Bitcoin network, namely the users patronizing the technology, should have to balance these two functions to allow bitcoin to grow as a currency. They would have to know when they need to hold on to their bitcoins, and they should also be wise enough to know when they should let it go and allow it to circulate in the network. If the hoarding of bitcoins continues and possibly worsen, it is not hard to imagine that people would recognize it as a currency to scarce and hard to grab a hold of that bitcoin would soon lose its purpose as a medium of exchange.

3. Pros to Bitcoins

Security

Quite possibly, bitcoin's biggest appeal to users is its close to nothing security breaches. If someone tries to hack a bank or robs a business, the moment the robber gets a hold of the safe or cash register then that day's profits could be considered down the drain. In contrast, since Bitcoin does not use any tangible currency should an attacker get a hold of a user's private keys, that attacker does not really gain any value since the original user would always have control over the private keys. Critics of Bitcoin would point out that these wallets and transactions are not entirely safe from security breaches. Maybe due to its young nature in the business, no massive hack has still ever been reported but should one ever occur then there would be no remedy for the users.

Lower fees

On average, credit card fees would be from 5-30% of the transaction, in comparison bitcoin transactions are lower than these. However, critics might argue that if you try adding costs for theft protection and other regulatory costs the final added cost for the transaction could be comparable to these fees.

Instantaneous transactions

Compared to conventional bank transfers or wire transfers and remittances that would normally take days to weeks for it to finally be settled and completed, bitcoin transactions are fulfilled almost instantaneously. But still, modern technology of money transfers and transactions, especially the use of online tools and smartphone apps, are all working better to also offer this close to real-time exchange of money.

Not only limited to currency

Since Bitcoin does not limit itself to only currency and you can basically take advantage of the open source code to transact the business, transfers are not only limited to money transfers but to other digital assets as well. This innovation opens a door of unlimited possibilities such as exchange of other contracts or specific applications to the users.

<u>Anonymity</u>

When performing transactions in the Bitcoin network, users can keep their identity anonymous by using pseudonyms or only using decrypted information about their identity. On the other end of the spectrum, transactions can also be performed with decreased privacy so that the users do not fall prey to the attack of hackers that are trying to access the complete financial information of the user by determining the address of the user.

4. Cons to Bitcoins

Too 'daunting' for ordinary users

Since Bitcoin technology prides itself with its complex blockchain backbone, many people who barely knows anything about programming and more so about the economics of money exchange might get easily intimidated by the technology. As a result, users might have to resort to the use of intermediaries that will be paid just for the sole purpose of making Bitcoin transactions clear to the clients. So, this might defeat the purpose of decreasing costs in the transactions. At some point, it may even be more of a burden than a convenience.

No credit

The United States of America, and most of the developed countries of the world, runs and functions under credits and credit scores. Unfortunately, Bitcoin still does not offer this credit option to its clients. Supporters, however, argue that this option could easily be incorporated into their transactions, users just must tailor fit this service into their system.

Volatility

Fiat currencies are managed by central banks and there are authorities making sure that the value continues to be stable. Bitcoin does not have this form of backup. Thus, the price and value of bitcoin is heavily in mercy of its users and transactions, which could be an advantage on itself but the moment things get downhill and a huge crack is made within the system, this could mean a massive blow to the stability of the system. As such, this appears to be the most vulnerable aspect of Bitcoin.

Bitcoin in business

Bitcoin has been created primarily to address the costs of conducting payment transactions. Here in this chapter we shall look at some of the first round of and most common business applications of bitcoin.

Since this is a recent form of technology, we still haven't begun to see the wide range of applications that Bitcoin technology could be applied into. We are still scratching at the surface of the endless possibilities of Bitcoin use but the list in this chapter will showcase the dynamics bitcoin has provided into the mode of transaction for these businesses.

1. Money transfer

The World Bank averages the money transfer fees in remittance centers or companies in the range of about 10%. In contrast, common Bitcoin transactions are only 0.01% to 0.05%, a huge slash by about a hundred from the average transfer fee we pay in transaction fees! Theoretically, Bitcoin has the advantage when it comes to cost of money transfer, but there are some reasons as to why this cost advantage may also be restricted for Bitcoin users.

Much of the costs for money transmittance goes into the administrative and regulatory costs of the transaction. The clients get to pay for these costs. It is presumed that as bitcoin gets larger and the startup business patronizing it gets more successful with larger clientele, then the business will have to eventually start charging their clients as well just to keep the business going.

One other caveat of money transfer is the availability of the right kind of technology that allows for Bitcoin transactions. Not all countries may have the same technological advancement that would make Bitcoin convenient, so this limits the client pool for money transfer and possibly to compensate for this disadvantage the Bitcoin transmitter may have to pay more just to accommodate cases for these countries.

Conversely, the limitation for technology could also transcend to limitation in the liquidity of Bitcoin to the local fiat currency. This would greatly increase money transfer cost just because very little converters recognize Bitcoin.

Still, supporters could see the potential of Bitcoin in the money transfer business. Especially considering the public ledger that creates transparency in the transaction where small businesses don't have to be heavily invested in their own personal means of creating security since Bitcoin already did that for them.

Utilizing Bitcoin in the massive remittance market is still a hot area of discussion, especially since its sustainability is still uncertain.

2. Exchanges

The exchanges, like foreign exchange markets, allows for the conversion of bitcoins into fiat money. Foreign exchanges, especially for the major currencies of the world such as US dollars, British pounds, and Japanese yen, are highly dynamic. Changing values almost every second.

The way these exchanges occurs is usually via a third-party model where a user would deposit their funds under a certain currency, an exchange is initiated and processed to account for the other denomination's value. The funds are kept in the user's account and only when the user orders for a withdrawal of the funds do they finally leave the exchange.

The way to make these exchanges using bitcoins is to also deposit the fund into a third-party model, thus leaving the blockchain recording system. The widespread practice of Bitcoin users is to keep the funds in the storage and only allow a certain small proportion of their funds in the wallets so that they would have direct control over it. Exchanges using bitcoin can be done by signing arbitrary messages using the private keys and transferring these funds from one address to another.

3. Web wallets

This system is a different system than the Bitcoin wallet, in fact this business is profiting by masking all the complexities of managing Bitcoin wallets for first-time users to utilize the technology without being daunted by its complexities. The way it works is quite like how online banking would work. Users would be requested to create an account online and deposit their bitcoins with the web wallet service. All payments and transactions would then be performed via the Web Wallet provider's platform and website. This convenience is not the only advantage web wallets provide their users. Web wallets also, like online banks, alert a user whenever there is a breach in the security of his or her wallet. Through their record tracking, web wallets could also warn a user in an event that the user is about to transact with another user with poor reputation. Web wallet services could protect their clients from possibly transferring bitcoins to bogus addresses intended to mislead users. Web wallets also allows users to link their accounts to their bank accounts.

As you can see there are a lot of risks for these services as well, most important of these is trusting all your information to new businesses (given the newness of Bitcoin technology) that are of higher risk of security breach. They are of course of higher risk since they are prized targets from attackers. Users must be very wary of putting all their eggs in one basket, and most especially wary of the web wallet service providers that they are choosing.

4. Mining

Bitcoin mining industry is any type of business that would secure the proper and secure functioning of the Bitcoin network. Different business models that are under this big Bitcoin industry includes the equipment manufacturers, such as companies that would design and distribute the actual hardware for Bitcoin technology. The developers of processors and the chip manufacturers. They all benefit greatly as the Bitcoin industry continues to expand. As final equipment gets produced by the manufacturers, data centers then start hosting this equipment. Datacenters also profit from Bitcoin mining. The people who run the mining hardware- the Bitcoin miners –

directly profit from this business and earning from block rewards. Directly managing these miners are mining pool operators who function as managers that allows for the smooth transactions of rewards to miners. The Bitcoin mining has indeed improved greatly that more specific positions and equipment are being utilized to keep this industry going.

5. ATMs

Automated Teller Machines for Bitcoin functions like conventional ATMs but instead of dispensing cash it functions the other way around where users can buy or sell bitcoins with cash. The procedure of operating a Bitcoin ATM pretty much follows the following steps:

User scans her ID and waits for the ATM to verify it.

User inputs cash and presents ATM with a QR code (usually generated by a Bitcoin wallet online or on a smartphone) that holds information about the user's public address.

ATM sends the purchased bitcoins into the directed address.

The way these ATMs profits is through the operation fee which is usually within the 3% – 7% range. Early users of Bitcoin ATMs were usually the curious users who were simply intrigued with the technology but now supporters have seen its value for travelers who could carry the bitcoins anywhere they go and simply exchange it to local currency in their destination country.

many banks are approaching Libra cautiously, citing regulatory uncertainty. Regulations around How to Store Bitcoins and Other Cryptocurrencies

When you have fiat currencies, you can store them in your wallet, at a bank, or even under the mattress if you so wish. When it comes to storing cryptocurrencies, while we have touched on Bitcoin wallets, which is what you use to store cryptocurrencies such as Bitcoin, we have not fully-fleshed this, which is not good because they are a few things you need to know about Bitcoin storage.

When you have Bitcoins, you store them in a wallet, which put simply, is an address on the blockchain. Each Bitcoin wallet has two keys: a private key, which we discussed earlier, and a public key. The public keys is the address those intending to send Bitcoins to you shall use while as indicated earlier, the private key is much like a password to the safe that has your funds. If you expose your private key, you may be the victim of a hack and lose all your money:

Now that we are talking about wallets, let us talk about the various wallet options at your disposal:

1. **Online Wallet:** An online wallet is the easiest way to store your Bitcoin. Here is a **list of online Bitcoin wallets to choose from**. That said, because the online space is prone to hacking, online wallets may not be the most secure or ideal for long-term storage for your Bitcoins.

2. Mobile Wallet: **A mobile wallet is a bit more secure than an online wallet as long as no one hacks your phone or your phone breaks (if any of these happens, your coins will be no more). For this option, you can download any of** these mobile wallets for your iOS device.

3. **A Desktop Wallet:** This wallet is similar to the mobile wallet with the only difference being that in this case, the wallet is for desktop computers. **Here is a list of such wallets for your choosing**.

4. **Hardware Wallets:** Hardware wallets are hardware devices specifically built to store Cryptocurrency keys. Because they are electronic—most resemble a flash drive—while safer than most of the other wallet we have discussed, they have their fair share of susceptibility. Here is a **list of various hardware wallets for your consideration**.

5. **Paper Wallet:** Paper wallet, which is where you store your private keys on paper, are the most secure from hacking. However, as is the case with most paper, you should store your paper wallet in a secure place and instead of using print paper, use terraslate paper. Here are **best practices for paper wallet**.

Having discussed this, let us continue with our earlier discussion:

In some instance, the input and output amount will not match. Because Bitcoins only exist as transactions, your Bitcoin address may end up with different transactions because each transaction is separate and the blockchain cannot combine the transactions to form one file for all the transactions.

In such a case, if you want to send a specific amount of Bitcoins, your wallet will attempt to use transaction records that amount to the amount of dollars you want to send. If your transaction history lacks the exact number of Bitcoins you want to send—perhaps you want to send 1.5 Bitcoins—and no two transactions amount to the amount you want to send, since you cannot split a transaction into the exact amount you want to send, you will have to transact the whole output. You will have to send one of the incoming transaction specifying how much you want to send, and then your wallet will return the excess to you as change.

For instance, if you send an incoming transaction of 2 Bitcoins, your wallet will create two output amounts for the transaction: one output for the 1.5 Bitcoins you want to send, and 0.5 Bitcoins to address the wallet (we are talking about an online or mobile wallet here) to hold the change.

You may also be wondering, "What about charges? Do I have to pay for these transactions?"

Transaction fees will vary depending on various factors. If a transaction has a portion not picked up by the recipient or returned as change to the sender, it automatically becomes a transaction fee. This fee goes to the miner who solves the transaction. Many are the instances where since miners are now processing transactions at no fee, you will not pay a thing.

Another thing you should know is that you can send parts of a Bitcoin. A satoshi is 1/100,000,000 of a Bitcoin. On the Bitcoin network, it is possible to transfer amounts as low as 5430 satoshis.

How Bitcoin Mining Works

In fiat currencies, when governments want to exercise fiscal prudence, they simply print more money. In Bitcoin, printing of money is not possible and instead, computers around the world compete to discover or mine Bitcoins. Here is how this happens:

When users within the Bitcoin network send transactions, the network collects all transactions made within a period into a block, which is, essentially, a list of transactions. Miners then confirm those results and write them to the ledger.

The ledger or blockchain contains a list of all transactions made between all Bitcoin addresses since the inception of the Bitcoin network. Whenever miners create a new block of transactions, they add it to the blockchain and everyone who participates in the Bitcoin network gets an updated copy of this so they can know about all transactions happening within the Bitcoin Network.

Miners also perform the critical task of maintaining the integrity of the blockchain. After the creation of a block of transactions, miners extract the information in the block and apply a mathematical formula that turns it into a hash, a shorter random sequence of numbers. They then store the hash with the block at the end of the blockchain.

Hashes ensure integrity of the Bitcoin system in that while it is possible to produce a hash from a Bitcoin block, working out the data by looking at the hash is impossible and because each hash is unique, changing a single character from a Bitcoin block will alter the entire hash.

To generate the hash, on top of the using the transactions in a block, miners also use the hash of the block last stored on the blockchain. Because the creation of each block's hash is somewhat dependent on the hash of the block before it, this acts as a wax seal in that blocks confirm the legitimacy of the block before them, which makes the block tamper proof.

If someone tried to fake a transaction by changing the a block already stored in a blockchain, the hash of that block would change and if one of the miners checked the authenticity of the block by running the hashing function, that miner would notice the difference in the new block and the block stored with the blockchain.

Further, because the production of a hash is dependent on the hash of the block before it, tampering with one block means all subsequent blocks will have flawed hashes with the process continuing down the chain.

The work of miners is to seal off a block, which they do by competing against each other using special hardware and software specifically designed for block mining. Whenever a miner successfully creates a hash, he or she gets 25 Bitcoins, and because this update reflects on the blockchain, everyone hears about it. This works as an incentive to keep recording transactions and mining.

This, as you can see, means it is rather easy to produce a hash from a collection of data, something computers are fairly good at. If mining were that simple, everyone would be doing it, which is why the Bitcoin network makes hashing harder: it does so by introducing something called proof-of-work (we discussed this in passing earlier).

The Bitcoin network/protocol does not accept any hash. The hash of a block has to look a certain way and have a specific number of zeros at the start. It is impossible to tell the nature of a hash before its production, and if a miner includes any new piece of data to the hash, the hash changes completely.

Now that we have understood everything cryptocurrencies and Bitcoins, let us look at how the blockchain technology, the underlying technology behind most cryptocurrencies, is shaping the future of money.

Chapter 3: Possible future development of Libra in the world

Retail

Libra would be a retail market made up of individuals and merchants who purchase products and services. Even though they are very big, retail markets, like wholesale markets, do not have the ability to destroy economic stability. Regulators should be interested: economic crises always begin in the unregulated industry, and Libra will be a gigantic shadow bank in effect. But if regulators worry about the impact of Libra on economic stability, they have a solution already. Force Facebook to become a controlled bank, like all other banks, subject to capital and liquidity demands.

Trading

Calibra will offer you the opportunity to send Libra as efficiently and in a flash to almost anyone with a cell phone as you can send an instant message at low to no price. Moreover, in time, we would like to give additional administrations for people and organizations, such as paying bills by pushing a catch, buying some espresso with the code output, or riding your neighboring open travel without expecting to transport cash or a metro pass.

Not at all like Bitcoin, the value of Libra is connected to an formally approved cash such as the dollar— explicitly to "a market-esteem box of a few in currency norms," Wired says. That's one of several distinct ways that Libra will try to keep a strategic distance from Bitcoin's unusual, shifty, betting atmosphere and various digital currencies. This isn't a coin you're buying since you think it's going to develop as lucrative various times. It is gradually comparable to trading for a euro with a dollar.

Financial systems

It is safe to say that the effect of Libra on the Financial System would be as large as that earlier outlined by the backers of the project. This fresh development alarms economic regulators, banks, and public officials.

Depending on who you're talking to, the reason individuals are either thrilled or worried is that Facebook has 2.4 billion customers globally. 1.7 billion of their customers have no bank accounts, which makes Libra highly appealing for remittances.

Know Your Customer (KYC) implications

Libra seems to target nations with lots of Facebook users and volatile currencies in particular— the other meaning of unbanked banking. There are apparent dangers of money laundering. Libra will have to maintain this tight and guarantee developed-world regulators that it has done so, or risk the entire Libra scheme. But this carries with it another danger: the local economy's potential liberalization. Just as unplanned dollarization— the domination of U.S. dollars — can lead to crippling local currency depreciation, so could Libra — but quicker. This will be most detrimental to those local residents who are unable to pass KYC controls on access to the Libra scheme; it establishes a Libra economy that only operates for the local middle to upper classes and wealthy tourists.

What is a smart contract?

This is the kind of contract that is self-executing without the need for third-party involvement, and the benefits of the contract automatically accrue to the parties in the contract. Let's look at a simple example.

Imagine a car rental agency where you book your car online, provide them with payment information using the crypto-based Ethereum platform. But the amount is not released; it is placed into a binding contract. The contract is for you to do one of two things: pick up the car, or cancel it before a certain time. The contract is placed within a condition in a short program. No payment is made but you are given a four-digit code, the plate number of the car and the lot where it is parked (the exact lot is known because the sensors on the car know exactly which lot the car is parked in). When you arrive at the airport, you go straight to that lot, find the car, and on the door is a keypad where you key in that number. The car unlocks, you have taken possession of the vehicle, and the crypto agreed to in the contract is transferred to the rental company. You get to drive off with the car. No standing in line. No last-minute changes, no hassles. No problems with a credit card, and the contract that was pre-agreed upon gets executed effortlessly and without any form of human intervention.

Think about that for a minute. Think about the savings in terms of labor and infrastructure. This car rental company can be located at any parking garage without having the need to pay for an office or people to staff that office. Contemplate a company like Hertz and the amount of money they pay in rental at airports across, let us say, just 200 major airports. Now remove that entire cost from their expenses.

That cost savings will result in cheaper services across the board. Not just in car rental, but also with individual businesses on a much smaller scale.

Think of the blockchain as part of the architecture for distributed storage services. There are already efforts to develop this beyond just the file storage that is available today. But the development of the decentralized blockchain to be used for storage will result in a robust distribution of parts of files that someone has.

Take for instance the fact that there are hundreds of millions of exabytes on personal computers and laptops around the world.

Imagine being able to take advantage of all that unused space to distribute a file stored in a decentralized way. More decentralized than cloud servers. You see, the problem with cloud servers is that they are moving in the wrong direction according to the future. While the rest of the world is moving towards decentralization, cloud storage is partially moving to centralization. Even though the cloud servers are segmented and fragmented, they are still concentrated in nodes that are in silos. If you use storage on a blockchain and utilize BitTorrent technology—a combination of blockchain, encryption and decentralized features along with BitTorrent downloading ability—you will have bits and pieces of your confidential file encrypted. Plus, they'll be broken up and stored in multiple locations so that when you go to download them off the blockchain, it pulls the data from multiple locations and decrypts them for your use.

The benefit of this is not just the ability to store data offline. Having blockchain storage will also allow you to keep your documents secure so they won't be able to be erased or destroyed. Imagine if your hard drive gets fried, or if your server is subjected to a nuclear pulse (in this day, anything is possible) your data gets erased. But what happens when you have copies of your data spread across multiple ledgers across the entire global network? The chance that your data gets destroyed or changed becomes extremely low.

The other development that needs to happen with the blockchain is that some sort of proof of work or proof of stake be devised and developed. The issue is really about spending something in return for something. In the case of the POW that Bitcoin uses in its processes for block creation, it requires huge amounts of computing power which takes a tremendous amount of energy to accomplish. The future development of blockchains needs to make sure that the energy-dependent nature is something less intensive. Ethereum, for one, has decided to use POS in its computational work. POS is proof of stake where the owners of Ethereum coins will be allowed to mine the blocks, and then the probability that are allowed to mine would be the ratio of the coin ownership to the ownership of the pool in general.

The blockchains must develop a better way of providing authentication to the mining system without the necessity of using large amounts of energy to do it. It is also possible to eventually use processing power from green electricity to conduct the mining.

Blockchains are also under review to be a part of the energy infrastructure. The use will allow energy companies to be decentralized, and a significant reduction in infrastructure and labor is expected. In the event this happens, it is possible that the energy needed to run the system could be attached to the energy producers.

The other option would be to choose proof of stake over proof of work as discussed. There is also the possibility of introducing some other form of investment into the blockchain environment. If you look at the proof of work or the proof of stake, you'll see a dynamic of return-driven activity. To be able to mine under POS criteria, you would have to purchase the coin. To be able to mine under the POW criteria, you would have to invest in the equipment. In either case, you need to invest in something, so that you are, in the end, a stakeholder.

The future of blockchains depends on finding the proper balance of the investment required to entice those who wish to advance as miners.

The other problem that is an issue with blockchains such as Bitcoin, is that they are susceptible to companies pooling their hashing power. At first glance, that does not look like a bad thing, until you recall something called the Fifty-one Percent Rule. This rule is all about the number of blocks that are confirmed by the nodes as a percentage of the nodes in the network. It is done by consensus, remember? If 51% of the nodes in a network agree to a block, then that is the block that takes on validity. Anyone having more than 51% of hashing power in a blockchain network should be a red flag. In the case of Bitcoin's blockchain, two companies have 53% of the total hashing power. This is a situation that is ripe for collusion and the cornering of the market in the event such an opportunity should arise.

There are pools that have miners who sign up with them and they (the administrators) control what happens. This makes me uneasy, and the development of blockchain technology should find a way of taking care of potential problems that arise from this. Besides, pools like this bring tremendous hashing power and promote that power to a point that the difficulty keeps escalating, and so the total power keeps going up just to produce the same output of work. This certainly needs to change.

The next development of the blockchain includes the introduction of AI - Artificial Intelligence, Smart Learning and Machine Learning into the blockchain. Most tech thinkers are excited about the prospect of this combination of two of the next generation's ideas merging.

The development of such a combination is already underway and aside from a few small initiatives, there isn't much to write home about just yet. However, it is pretty certain that within the next five to ten years the AI/Blockchain combination will attain a strong footing in the world, and that will cause the shift in how we live our lives. We are already seeing the Internet of Things changing the way Blockchain is used. We will then see how Big Data is passed and stored, then comes the amalgamation of the technologies that will allow for human beings and the civilization we live in to take the biggest leap yet.

The Internet of Things

If you haven't heard of the IoT, let me just give you a brief review of it. The IoT is about being able connect all equipment and electronics, from your fridge, to your watch, sunglasses, car, toaster—everything. Once you tag all of these things and put them on to the internet, you will be able to control them in any way from anywhere. The Internet of things is designed to connect devices the way social media connects humans (not in the exact same way, but you get the point).

The development of the blockchain technically has the potential to be the platform to connect devices around the world to our own device, without us worrying that it could get hacked. Wearable computing meeting big data will inadvertently land us all in AI territory. Keeping the blockchain (or some more advanced from of it) will move this along faster and further in a shorter period of time.

Blockchain holds the key to being resilient to DDOS attacks and to be able to overcome virus attacks as well as malware issues. As you have seen in other parts of the book, the blockchain can be designed to be impervious to the typical bad actor. It is also easy hide in the cloud, break up the footprint and scatter it across the blockchain.

The internet of things gives as a great way to further the power of the blockchain to be not only part of the nodes but also the tools which make it impervious to attacks.

Different Blockchains

There are numerous blockchains across different architectural formats written in numerous programming languages. There are a string of them that you can download from GitHub. There are also blockchains that are varied in nature and objective, and you can get just about anyone who can use some sort of object-oriented programing to create a new blockchain with your objective in mind. Blockchains are the results of programing parameters and processes, not a physical architecture that needs to be built with physical materials.

But for now there are three special blockchains that I want to look at in particular and they all have to do with cryptocurrencies, tokens, and smart contracts. You see, the blockchain beneath the utility layer, as discussed earlier in the book, has some impact on how the blockchain below behaves. If it is just purely currencies like the Bitcoin network, then the mechanisms in place are a little different. If it's for smart contracts then the mechanism is a little different. Finally, if they are meant for tokens, then the structure is just a little different as well.

The currency blockchain can be divided into two main avenues—the bitcoin blockchain and the altcoin blockchain. Most of the blockchains require proof of work for the miners to be able to have a shot at the rewards. Then comes the Ethereum blockchain that is optimized for the transmission of smart contracts. And finally there is the blockchain that manages tokens like that of Filecoin. I will get into the last two in turn, as we have already exhaustively looked at bitcoin earlier.

Blockchain vs Hashgraph

The one thing that should start becoming apparent is that the blockchain is not just attached at the hip to any particular cryptocurrency. Even more than that, the blockchain is not exclusive to Bitcoin. Bitcoin indeed does have its blockchain, but it must be fully understood that the blockchain is totally malleable and can be designed to support almost anything that it needs to on top of it. The blockchain in essence becomes the platform for the application that's added on top of it. In between the application and the platform of the blockchain, are the tokens or cryptos that facilitate the connection and bring monetary or currency value between the two layers.

There have been multiple attempts to 'alter' the role of the blockchain, but in effect what people are really doing is altering the format of the blockchain, not the concept of it. One such situation is the development of the Hashgraph. It is seen as the possible replacement to the current format of the blockchain.

Hashgraph is what they call a distributed ledger with consensus algorithm. They have gone through great pains to not call it blockchain and there is a reason for that. First of all you have to remember that Satoshi never patented the blockchain. The developer of Hashgraph, Leemon Baird, did however, patent Hashgraph. And so if he wanted to patent it, it had to be unique. Therefore, there are a few things he has done to differentiate it which worked really well. But it is in essence another blockchain.

Let me give you an idea of how the Hashgraph system works (since they don't want to call it a blockchain, I shall respect their wishes). Hashgraph does indeed do a few things better than the traditional blockchain. For one, it does not allow the miners to pick and choose which transaction it wants to include in a block. It all has to be included based on the timestamp. If you recall, miners now have the right to choose who they include in their block when it comes to the current bitcoin block. That is obviated in the Hashgraph version. So that's a good thing. In the event you are planning to create your own blockchain, this is probably something that you would want to do.

So the first similarity between Hashgraph and Blockchain are that they both use a form of gossip protocol. But the difference is that the events are properly timed, and the timed events are not based on what each node says but on the consensus algorithm that runs Hashgraph. So no one can cheat on the time. Also, because there is a fairness protocol in Hashgraph, you get a sense of certainty that a transaction is going to get included in the 'block' regardless of the tip that the transaction participants provide. In bitcoin there is a tipping mechanism where participants provide a fee in the transaction to be given to the miners. Miners have the habit of taking that fee into consideration when they mine the blocks. They tend to leave out transactions that have little or no additional fees and take the ones that have the higher fees.

That's the key difference between Hashgraph and Blockchain. One more thing. Even though they both use gossip protocols, Hashgraph goes one step further and produces gossip about gossip. So that's a little different, in the sense that there are gossips which create events that are not really material events. It means that if A talks to B, that is an event, even if there is no material transaction. The moment A talking to B creates an event, it means that B can now tell C that there was an event of A talking to it. And so now they keep talking about talking. And they do this very rapidly. Smaller packets of events, each containing the time stamp, are passed along. That works great because then what happens is that the Hashgraph is able to keep a timestamp of its own in consensus. When you have a thousand people all with their clocks slightly off, pile over and over again over aen event, there is no way that event is something that happened in the future, so the mistaken (or intentionally altered time stamp) problem is solved in the Hashgraph.

Between the time stamp issue and the way they take transactions it becomes a fairer process. In this case it also becomes a faster process, because the more people there are in the network, the faster the gossip rate becomes and that means that the transaction rate is also faster. Hashgraph claims that it can do more than 50,000 transactions per second compared to Bitcoin's significantly lower number. This is really good news, and if and when you get to develop your own blockchain, these are the things you want to think about.

Not only is Hashgraph fair, it is also cheaper and faster, with the ability to perform more transactions. The developers are also advancing the process to be quantum tolerant.

Blockchain vs Tangle

The Tangle is an interesting version of the blockchain to a certain extent. It takes all the things that work well in the blockchain and improves things by removing some of the aspects that are not needed, while enhancing some of the parts that are needed. For instance, there are no fees and there are no miners. The fact that blockchains use miners makes it impossible to do anything without them, because without miners it is impossible to keep the transactions in blocks and to verify them. However, the idea of being able to tip the miner should not have been something that was ever implemented, as there should not have been fees at all. The block reward should have been more than enough to be able to incentivize the miners. But because it started that way, it is now very difficult to change that and as a result, it is impossible to send microtransactions.

In the case of Tangle there are no blocks, so that means there are no miners. If there are no miners then there are no fees. So far so good. But the most important thing is that it does use distributed consensus. It also offers quantum security which means it can't be ranked when quantum computers become mainstream. Tangle also offers scalability, so that is a very good start. It is something that you might want to consider when you try to develop your own blockchain or wish to fork the code here as well.

Tangle uses what we call a DAG—A Directed Acyclic Graph. It's easy to unpack. Directed means it just goes in one direction and Acyclic tells us that it is linear and noncircular, so it does not go over itself.

The beauty about this sort of blockchain (and again, they do not like being called a blockchain, they call the foundation a tangle) is that they do not need the miners to accumulate transactions; each transaction is verified by two transaction after it and it is done so, randomly.

Let me give you a few terms to play with so that you get a little better understanding of the tangle. The coin that is built on the tangle, by the way, is the IOTA. The tangle doesn't use blocks. Instead it uses transactions that need to be verified by two transactions that happen after it. Each transaction is not called a block, but a site. When a site is created, two sites randomly chosen behind it will verify the first site. Then four other transactions will verify the last two transactions, and that keeps going downstream. The two sites that are verified are chosen by the system using a random algorithm so that no one person can keep approving his or her own transactions. As the sites approve each other, the line of sites form "branches"—so called because they form a crooked or jagged line from the tips to the ends. The tips are the most recent sites that have yet to have any transaction confirm them.

By doing it in this way, what happens is that the scalability rides on itself. The more people there are, the faster the transactions get done. And instead of the blockchain getting jammed because the miners are trying to choose who is paying them more and the fact that each block has a 1MB limit, it is much less chaotic in the world of Tangle than it is in the Bitcoin blockchain.

Chapter 4: The Libra and Block chain

Let's take Bitcoin as an example. The best way to understand the process of Bitcoin transaction registration is to follow step-by-step guidance. When a user wants to send bitcoins to someone else, they broadcast the details of the transaction – their public key, the recipient's public key, and the bitcoin amount transferred – to a network of interlinked nodes.

Most popular cryptocurrencies and why they matter?

Bitcoin (BTC)

To start off — Bitcoin. It is the market's first and strongest cryptocurrency. Created by the anonymous Satoshi Nakamoto in 2009, it brought digital money to the globe. Bitcoin's critics criticized it for all — its speed and elevated transaction charges. So, it's not the finest currency for its functionality, by no means. However, it is still one of the most precious and strong digital currencies despite its various issues. Many experts compare Bitcoin to digital gold. Meaning that although it is not the best way to buy or make micro-transactions, its key function is to store value, online gold. Imagine buying bread. You would have to use gold (Bitcoin) to buy it. Instead, use fiat currency, or other cryptocurrencies.

Ethereum (ETH)

It's the second strongest and most famous cryptocurrency today, shortly known as Ether. It's not just a currency that makes Ether different. It is a platform based on blockchain that allows you to create apps and projects. While, Bitcoin is used only for more standard operations.

Unique benefit of using Ethereum is that it has a devoted team that operates on currency growth and a unified community unlike Bitcoin. Within the society, people agree in which direction they want to carry Ether, making it more stable and quicker solution.

IOTA (MIOTA)

Although IOTA has significantly dropped in value over the past months, it does not take away its uniqueness. Being established in 2015, it is the only electronic currency not using blockchain technology. It is constructed using 'Tangle' scheme. The currency has concentrated on constructing a technology that can be used in the' Internet-of-Things' (IoT) age for transactions. If you're not acquainted with it, IoT is a technology that would allow communication across the Internet between objects that have sensors. In other words, IOTA sees itself as the future's cryptocurrency.

Ripple (XRP)

Ripple wants to fix International Payment Transfer issues. It focuses primarily on making global digital payments cheaper and quicker, unlike other currencies. What also distinguishes it from other currencies is the fiat that founds 50% of the total supply of XRP. It is uncommon because decentralization is one of the primary principles of digital currencies.

Blockchain Potential in the Non-Financial Sector

Now that we have looked a major way that blockchain could potentially be used in the financial sector through stock market implementation, it's time to look at the ways that blockchain could influence non-financial institutions. Before we dive into this chapter and look at any specific ways the blockchain can influence the non-financial sector, it's important to take a step back and look at a key element of blockchain. Even though so far, we have only talked about blockchain from the perspective of currency exchange, the prowess of blockchain has to do more with defining ownership than anything else. Blockchain is able to organize who owns what and when, while also being able to provide information on who owned what previously and how much of it was owned. This idea of ownership is where the non-financial aspects of blockchain potential is headed. This chapter will look at what Ethereum and Smart Contracts are and how these applications are both using blockchain as a way to prove individual ownership within their respective networks.

Build Your Own Blockchain with the Help of Ethereum

Ethereum is an open-source network that seems to have taken the basic points of the bitcoin application and expanded on them. Within Ethereum, you're able to build your own blockchain database. A key feature of Ethereum is the fact that you are able to trade internationally on its platform, via its EVM. EVM stands for Ethereum Virtual Machine. If you were to decide that you wanted to build your own blockchain platform using Ethereum, here is a list of some of the things you could do:

Create your own currency. The currency that is inherent to Ethereum is known as Ether; however, once you open up your own blockchain network on the Ethereum platform, you have the ability to create a currency that is completely unique to your blockchain network.

Operate your own market. Let's say that you sell your own products on the Internet. A blockchain network would allow you to completely centralize your product and develop an online marketplace for yourself that does not require dependence on Amazon or another super corporation. You would be completely in charge of how your market is run.

Keep track of where your money is going. Your blockchain network on the Ethereum platform would allow you to keep track of the debts that people owe you along with your profitability.

Although we will get to what Smart Contracts are later in this chapter, Ethereum also allows you to develop contracts with people on your network. This allows you to prove who owns what.

Ethereum also allows their users to process ownership in the case of death. This includes the fulfillment of wills or other types of death documents where ownership needs to be processed to someone else.

As you can see, Ethereum has been developed to go beyond the capabilities of a single bitcoin system. You can think of Ethereum as being able to provide you with the capability to start your own digital marketplace. Instead of subscribing to an already operational network (such as what you do on a platform such as Etsy or eBay), you are truly calling the shots and controlling your interaction with your customers. This is a real consumer innovation that would not be possible without the Internet or blockchain methodology. The Ethereum application makes it pretty clear that society has not reached its full blockchain potential.

Declaring Ownership with Smart Contracts

At its core, the application of the Smart Contract allows people to trade ownership of goods or services without having to meet in person. This concept was developed by the developed Nick Szabo. At first, this concept may not seem like it would be particularly beneficial, but you may change your mind after it's put into perspective a bit. For example, if you have ever tried to purchase a home before, you already know that there are many aspects to the home buying process. When you purchase a home, you have to contact your bank, a mortgage lender, a realtor, a lawyer, and the selling agent as well. You also need a home inspector and potentially other types of people such as mold removal experts or asbestos removal experts. It's safe to say that this process can become complex quickly. If you're unorganized, the potential for a headache of a time is pretty high.

These complicated processes are the types of circumstances that the notion of a Smart Contract seeks to rectify. It uses blockchain technology to allow multiple enterprises to see the progress of contract completion, as long as access is granted to these different entities. Another way to think about how a Smart Contract works is to consider it as being similar to a checklist. Let's take the example of buying a house. When you buy a house, just a few of the documents that you will need to verify and present on the day of closing include down payment amount, any completion items that the seller has agreed to rectify for you, and documents that a lawyer will need you to sign to make the sale final. When these items are online and in a digital format, all of the parties who are involved in the home buying transaction are able to see the progress of these documents. Additionally, the seller and the buyer are able to sign their documents electronically, and a need for a sit-down meeting becomes obsolete. Smart Contracts allow for virtual roundtable interaction. This saves the entire process time and makes the entire home buying process easier for everyone involved.

If we go beyond the example of buying a home, it is also possible to see how a Smart Contract is largely more efficient than a traditional contract. For example, let's take the example renting an apartment. Let's say that you are a landlord. You're also rich, and you decide that you're going to spend your money by purchasing an apartment complex that can hold 20 residents. Obviously, managing 20 homes is going to be considerable work for you, especially when rent day comes.

A primary goal of a landlord is to get paid on time, yet so often, it seems as if a rent payment is late and the landlord is the one who has to carry the burden of this late payment. Of course, almost every rent contract has a stipulation in it regarding an additional cost that is accrued when a rent payment is late, but this late fee is not always tacked onto the cost of rent for the month. We can all agree that this is a problem, especially for a landlord who needs to make ends meet each month.

A Smart Contract takes some of the responsibility of having to pester people for their rent payments from the landlord and places back on itself. If you were a landlord and decided to organize your individual leases using a Smart Contract network, this would mean that the Smart Contract would be automatically be able to determine when a tenant's rent was late. It would automatically be able to generate a late fee to the tenant's wallet as soon as the 1st of the month came and went, alleviating pressure from the landlord to track down the tenant and demand payment. With a Smart Contract, the algorithms that are built into the network use "if", "and", and "or" statements in order to figure out when certain stipulations need to occur. The Smart Contract keeps tabs on the state of contract compliance. If a portion of the contract is violated, the Smart Contract takes immediate action.

The Advantages of Using a Smart Contract

Currently, there are a variety of advantages that are available to someone who opts to become a part of a Smart Contract network. One of these advantages is the idea that you are now able to combine Smart Contracts with use on your own Ethereum network if you wish to do so. Doing this allows you to make your Ethereum network even more efficient, depending on the venture or marketplace that you're trying to operate while using it. Let's take a look at some of the advantages that using a Smart Contract can provide an individual so that it's even more obvious as to why the future of all contractual obligations may take place using this type of digital ownership.

Advantage 1: More Efficient Transparency

If we go back to the example of the landlord using the Smart Contract system to make sure that he or she is getting paid on time, it is obvious that the Smart Contract is able to provide both the landlord and the tenant with optimum informational insight. Sticking to the notion of the public ledger but adapting it a bit, the Smart Contract allows visibility of the contract to be seen between both the tenant and the landlord. All members of any type of contract are able to interact with the contract together, and this makes accessibility of the contract easier for all of the parties who are involved. If the landlord of an apartment complex were to charge a late fee to a tenant's account, this late fee would immediately show on the contract ledger. The tenant would have no questions as to why they were charged more money, and it would be hard to dispute this charge when the explanation is as clear as day. The Smart Contract is able to optimize the idea of transparency, while keeping all aspects of a contract organized and succinct.

Advantage 2: Maintain Obligation

People get sued all of the time for a variety of reasons. One reason out of many is because of the fact that not everyone stays true to a contract that they initially sign. A Smart Contract makes it harder for someone to break a contract because of the fact that this type of contract is going to be tied to an individual's online presence. For example, it's likely that you are constantly bombarded with emails on the regular. Even if you don't like receiving the emails that are asking you to sign up for this or purchase that, it's almost impossible to completely rid yourself of this type of relentless advertising. With notifications that happen on a Smart Contract being directly connected to your identity within a computer, it will be easier than ever for a person with whom you're engaged in a contract to contact you or seek you out when you are in violation of something. This idea makes it obvious that the entire way in which people maintain their obligations to one another could change if Smart Contracts ever end up becoming popular or even replacing the traditional method of how contracts are kept. Remember, none of these considerations would be possible without the notion of the blockchain.

While the two main advantages to using Smart Contracts have been stated above, one disadvantage that still needs to be worked out includes keeping a contract private when needed. Most blockchain networks are transparent by nature; yet, it should be obvious that there are instances when a company may want to keep their business private for one reason or another. The kinks that surround the idea of privacy within a Smart Contract network are still being discussed; however, it should be apparent that this same problem keeps popping up in our blockchain examples.

The same problem regarding the super fund occurred in that network as well. The discussion of how much transparency is a good thing is one that may not have a solid or black-and-white answer. It's also not a question that will have the same answering, depending on who you ask. The amount of transparency that a marketplace should ideally have is an ethical question that has no "right" answer. This is why it's important that you as an individual keep an eye on how blockchain developers are answering this question.

Implications for the Future of Blockchain Technology

At this point in the book, it should be obvious that blockchain technology has the potential to completely revolutionize the way in which people and all of humanity interacts with their physical surroundings and infrastructures. The thought that one day you could potentially operate within a digital nation or digital town square has finally come to fruition, and its origins live in what blockchain has to offer. This chapter will look at the future of blockchain and how this type of technology could possibly be the wave of the future for many years to come from a technological and digital perspective.

Fintech and Its Future

Fintech is an abbreviated word that stands for "Financial Technology". We have already looked an example of fintech through our discussion of a blockchain platform that helps to operate the stock market, but there are many other networks that are out there that are both already developed and in the process of being developed. It's pretty easy to understand why fintech concepts would be important to banking institutions all over the world. No large banking corporation wants to become obsolete due to digital financial advancements, which is why so many of these institutions have already started to develop their own blockchain operational networks. For example, megacorporations such as Goldman Sachs and IBM have put a lot of money into developing blockchain networks from which their banks can operate. These banks hope that if and when blockchain technology takes over, their institutions will be safe from complete obliteration into nonexistence.

It's safe to say that there are two other reasons why banks have a large interest in developing blockchain networks of their own. The first reason has to do with trust. Obviously, trustworthiness is an essential quality that any bank must prove that they have to the public if they ever hope to have a lot of business. These days, people are more skeptical than ever before, and not everyone trusts the idea that a private bank is going to manage their money with the most altruistic interests in mind. Often, individuals within a privatized bank will act secretly selfish, in the hope that they will be able to yield higher dividends of profit. Along this line of thinking, if a big bank was able to say that they are now operating on a decentralized and transparent network, then this could make less of the public less skeptical about their operations and, thus, the bank could acquire more business for itself.

The second reason why a bank might have a vested interest in developing a blockchain network is because they can still potentially maintain privatization on the network, even though they are outwardly claiming that their network is open source. If everyone on the blockchain system that is owned by a bank works for the bank, then how is the idea of transparency truly maintained? This idea makes it necessary to step back and think about the implications of doing business with a bank that has been developed on a blockchain network. Unless you as an individual are able to log into the bank's blockchain network and see a public ledger of your fund activity for yourself, transparency as an ideal has been manipulated by the banks to be something that is less transparent and more controlled than is truly necessary on a blockchain network.

Blockchain and Use in the Government

As of February 2017, there was only one country that has taken concrete steps (so far) towards using blockchain technology in any serious way within society. This country was the Republic of Georgia. They approved legislation which stated that blockchain technology could be used as a way to prove ownership of land within its country's borders. Specifically, blockchain technology will now be used to authorize new land titles, trade ownership of land between people who are looking to buy and sell property, approve a situation where people are looking to demolish property that is on their own land, and provide services related to mortgage lending and housing endeavors. The Republic of Georgia is the first country to legally authorize the use of blockchain within its society, but it is safe to say that they will not be the last. Honduras and Sweden, just to name two, have also begun looking into how they can use blockchain within their respective societies.

The Future of Blockchain

The fact that an actual government has authorized the use of blockchain for municipal decisions in a society should be ultimate proof to you that blockchain is going to definitely have concrete influence in our world. If we think creatively for a minute, the potential for how our society could be influenced by blockchain is vast and complex. Of course, there are plenty of questions that come with this type of digital development, but these questions will surely be answered in time if blockchain technology is ever going to be considered a viable tool for the proof of ownership. As of right now, the potential for blockchain technology seems endless.

Even though the potential for blockchain seems endless, it is doubly important that society recognizes the great risks that come along with developing new types of technology and ways of currency exchange. Intrade.com, for example, did not adequately prepare itself for the speed at which their company would grow. This ultimately led to many people losing their money. The major risks that are currently associated with blockchain include questions regarding how insurance companies will operate within it, how currency will be valued properly, and how it can be regulated by the government. These important questions require that developers work both diligently and carefully to provide society with technology that is even safer than the physical institutions that are currently the pillars of how our societies operate.

Implications of Blockchain: Big Data, Privacy, and Personal Data

As we enter an increasingly digital age, many of the practices that were developed prior to the Internet have simply been applied to the new framework of a networked world. Instead of writing letters, we now send e-mails, for example. At face value, the process doesn't seem that all that different. In some cases, it isn't.

Regardless of how you may feel about it, there is no denying that more and more things are becoming integrated into the Internet, hence the aptly titled notion of the "Internet of Things" (often abbreviated to IoT). Devices like heart-rate monitors, self-driving cars, and even refrigerators are making their way into the market. Of course, almost everyone is already accustomed to carrying a smartphone around at all times, regularly checking GPS information, updating social media feeds, managing financial transactions, and much more.

Almost every area of life that one can think of is wired into the web already or has the potential to be in the near future. While there are many advantages to the burgeoning revolution in "smart technology," there are also some major concerns and challenges.

While it may seem like things like social media networks, smart toasters, and FitBits are entirely different ideas, they actually have quite a bit in common. Fundamentally, they all produce data: data about you. If you recall in the section on SHA-256, we noted that all digital data can ultimately be reduced to 0's and 1's. From that perspective, our heart rate and our Google search history are not ultimately all that different in terms. We all generate data constantly, whether it is telling Amazon's Alexa to order more paper towels, Googling pictures of baby sea lions, or tracking your workout schedule with an App or a wearable.

Where does this data go? Who **owns** this data? What can be learned about you by your trail of data? These questions quickly lead anyone bold enough to ask them into very uncomfortable territory. While getting to deep into the answer to this particular set of questions is beyond the scope of this book, it is worth scratching the surface. In short, there are huge multi-national companies that buy up your data and sell it to other companies. What do they do with it? Good question. Of course, they target ads based on your history. Sure. We all know that. What else, though? Part of what makes this avenue uncomfortable is that nobody really knows, and the space of data collection is loosely defined and loosely regulated.

Let's look at an example. Let's say, hypothetically, you found a little lump in your armpit one day. You are naturally a bit nervous, and you rush over to Google and spend several hours clicking around different websites to read articles about cancer. Now, let's say, hypothetically, that whatever company is sucking up your data gets their hands on this searching binge. Perhaps they also notice that you looked up a phone number for some doctor in the area who does cancer screenings. While you're at it, maybe it is time to start thinking about your health insurance policy, or to buy life insurance just in case?

Continuing the hypothetical situation, if an insurance provider were to buy your data, already parsed by some massive data broker, and see that you had been recently looking up information about cancer, what are the implications? Even if you have told nobody about the lump, even if you have not been evaluated by a doctor or diagnosed, could this potential insurer infer things from your data history when deciding on your premium rate, or whether to offer insurance to you at all?

This is just one example of a wide range of ethical and legal dilemmas that arise when we really begin thinking about the implications of our data, how it is mined, who "owns it," and who has access to it.

The more integrated technology becomes into society and all levels of life and the more pervasive networks become, the greater the volume and variety of data about all of us. What movies and music we stream, our shopping history, political leanings, sexual preferences, connections on social networks, devices we use, and much more is information that is often being collected as a result of blindly checking a user agreement box in order to use a particular service.

Ok, that's creepy, but what does it have to do with blockchain technology? Good question. The relationship between privacy and technology is an issue that spans many industries and contemporary debates.

For many enthusiasts of both cryptocurrencies and blockchain technology, privacy is a major concern. When it comes to the concept of "privacy," many observers, including major media outlets, make the assumption that "the only people who care about privacy are those with something to hide." This has led to a great deal of reporting on cryptocurrencies, in particular, suggesting that the primary appeal of these technologies is that they enable criminal activity. As more and more areas of life become connected to the Internet, it seems far-fetched to suggest that desiring more control over one's personal data, transactions, and asset management constitutes or implies criminal behavior. Many privacy advocates argue that privacy is essential to both individual welfare and a functional democracy.

Rather than relying on centralized institutions to provide services in exchange for ownership of our data, blockchain-based models are beginning to emerge that shift information to a secure, trustless, decentralized structure. ("Trustless" here means that participants do not need to put their trust in a centralized institution to mediate transactions, keep records, distribute wealth, store data, etc.).

The implications for blockchain in spaces like managing personal information, such as health records, are extremely promising and beginning to gain a lot of attention from investors, entrepreneurs, major corporations, and government entities.

Regardless of your feelings on the subject of privacy, it is worth noting, from an investment perspective, that several notable cryptocurrencies have emerged with an emphasis on privacy as a defining factor. The ability to make completely anonymous transactions that are also totally secure has elevated several currencies to the forefront of the cryptocurrency space, including Monero, ZCash, and Dash. While none of these have reached quite the height of Bitcoin or Ethereum in terms of widespread adoption, all three of these are among the top 50 cryptocurrencies in terms of market value. We can infer from their success that enough people see value in anonymity to make these currencies competitive players in the larger cryptocurrency market, as well as the general blockchain space.

Profiting from Blockchain Technologies

It is important to remember that blockchain technology is still very new. The implications of secure distributed ledgers and decentralized peer-to-peer systems of this variety are not yet fully realized. As with any frontier space, even in the digital realm, there are a lot of opportunities. Of course, the nature of frontiers is that they are unexplored territory, and where there is potential for opportunity there is also a higher risk factor than one might encounter in tamer and more regulated environments.

While much of the blockchain space is a "wild west," major players and industry leaders from numerous fields are beginning to invest in and explore blockchain technology. Big technology companies such as IBM and Microsoft are beginning to explore blockchains, along with numerous banks, particularly in Europe and Asia.

Even governments in many parts of the world are beginning to implement blockchains to manage public services and records. Estonia, for example, issues citizens cryptographically secure ID cards, managed by a blockchain, that allow access to various public services. The government of Georgia is using blockchain technology to manage land titles and validate property transactions. The UN recently completed a trial program using the Ethereum blockchain to manage distribution of food aid to 10,000 refugees.

Over the past few years, numerous hedge funds dealing in cryptocurrencies and blockchain applications have sprung up all over the world, and many Wall Street speculators have fixed their attention on the blockchain space. In 2016, Overstock, one of the largest online retailers in the US, released a blockchain-based platform for equities trading. Numerous startups have emerged that use blockchains to manage peer-to-peer micropayments at extremely low rates. In some cases, these enable international transfers and access to cash pickups, which allows unbanked individuals to send and receive payments.

New developments are happening on a daily basis in the blockchain space. For those interested in diving in, getting involved and profiting from these emerging technologies, the single most important thing you can do is to stay informed: Read white papers, join online communities, and explore the different projects gaining traction around blockchain technology. The more familiar you are with the space, the easier it will be to make informed decisions about which projects to invest in.

As a practical matter, broadly speaking, there are two general directions you can go in terms of investing in blockchain technology: cryptocurrencies and everything else. These are by no means mutually exclusive, and as we have seen with projects like Ethereum and Ripple, there is often some overlap between the two, or the integration of a digital token into a particular blockchain application.

Within the cryptocurrency space, active online marketplaces and exchanges exist with a trading culture similar to traditional stock exchanges. People trade fiat currency for cryptocurrencies as well as trading one cryptocurrency for another, striving to make a profit by investing in currencies that they think will increase in value.

Most cryptocurrency exchanges deal primarily in Bitcoin. In order to buy into other cryptocurrencies, you almost always need to have some Bitcoin to exchange, although some currencies and exchanges allow for a direct exchange between fiat and "altcoins," a common term for cryptocurrencies other than Bitcoin. You can buy Bitcoin through several online exchanges or from an increasing number of Bitcoin ATM's that are available in various locations throughout the world.

You may choose to actively trade between different cryptocurrencies, or simply buy into Bitcoin and/or altcoins that you believe are promising and hold on to them with the assumption that they will increase in value over time. This is one way to get involved with what is currently the most active environment for blockchain applications. If you're lucky, you could end up as an "early investor" in a technology that really takes off.

Many people have entered the cryptocurrency space with precisely that hope, especially after hearing about the success of Bitcoin. If you are new to blockchain-based digital currencies, it is important to understand that this is an extremely volatile space. It is not uncommon to see huge spikes and drops in value throughout the course of a few hours, while it is possible to make a lot of money if you play your cards right, it is also easy to lose money.

Being aware of the risks and making smart investments in cryptocurrencies is arguably the most direct route towards profiting from blockchain technology. It is certainly the easiest. For people that don't necessarily have much capital to invest, the prospect of mining can sound pretty appealing. We've already discussed some of the challenges associated with mining Bitcoin: you need to buy specialized equipment, electricity costs, the need for massive computing power, etc. If you're low on capital, investing in a Bitcoin mining operation is probably not the best option.

However, there are many other cryptocurrencies that can be mined with considerably less of a barrier to entry. For those who are willing to learn what it takes to convert a spare computer into a mining rig, the ability to earn coins through mining can be a potential way to generate passive income through validating blockchain transactions.

Blockchain technology originated in the cryptocurrency space, and much of the early development of blockchain applications has been in relation to digital assets and financial transactions. In terms of profiting from blockchain technology, becoming involved with cryptocurrencies is one popular avenue, but it is not the only gig in town. Increasingly, as blockchain finds its way into new fields, a savvy investor can find many fascinating offshoots that could very well grow into massive projects with global implications and take the future by storm. Investing in companies, developers, and technology that are exploring the possibilities of blockchain is gaining rapid popularity with everyone from Silicon Valley entrepreneurs to Wall Street executives.

Of course, nobody knows for certain which blockchain-based application will be "the next Google." Any potential investor will inevitably face the challenge of gauging which initiatives are over-hyped versus which are promising underdogs, which are revolutionary platforms versus cheap imitations. While there is no crystal ball that can predict the future, you can bolster your odds of picking a winner by doing research and asking the right questions. Some important questions to ask when considering whether a project has a good chance of success include:

- What problem does the technology solve (Does incorporating a blockchain actually make sense in this situation? Is this the best solution?)

- Is this project actually functional? Is it live and being used currently or is it an idea that has not yet been built? If it hasn't been built, how can you be sure that it will actually accomplish what it promises?

- How is the blockchain structured? (For example, if the founder controls 90% of the nodes on the network, what might that say about the company?)

- What is their consensus algorithm? Proof-of-Work? Proof-of-Stake? Something else? Why did they choose this system and how is it implemented.

- Is it scalable? Could this system meet the demands of a large user base?

- How does anonymity factor into this application? Is that significant?

- Is this platform secure? How is security guaranteed? Is there "trust" involved in a centralized body? What kind of encryption are they using?

- Is the blockchain open and visible to anybody?

- Is the project's code open-source? (If it's not, why not? How will we be able to determine how decisions are made, transactions are deemed valid, and exactly what is being executed when we use this platform?)

- Who is behind this project? Is the development team qualified and reputable? Have they been involved with previous projects that failed? Why did those fail?

- Are other projects doing something similar? What makes this one the best?

- Do you believe in this project? Are you excited about it?

This laundry list of questions is by no means exhaustive, but if you are thinking about investing serious money in blockchain technology these considerations are a good place to begin. With the increasing attention of several major industries aimed towards blockchain technology, it should not come as a surprise that many entrepreneurs have taken notice of the potential for big money in developing blockchain applications. Needless to say, not all of these applications are going to succeed and some are more promising than others. Some projects can be noble efforts that simply don't have the best solution to a common problem; others may be outright scams.

Take time to become familiar with the buzzwords and jargon of the blockchain space. When a new company claims to deliver a blockchain platform that is "100% scalable," a wise investor will likely ask exactly how they have managed to accomplish this, rather than taking the company's word at face value. More often than not, you may find that bold claims like "100% scalable" are closer to "future goals" than to the current reality.

It is no secret that marketing hype can play a huge role in how "popular" something becomes. Cryptocurrencies and blockchain-based companies are no exception, and marketing can have a real impact on how a player in this space is valued. Maybe a project lives up to the hype, but it is generally a good idea to approach potential investments in this space with a dose of healthy skepticism. Alternatively, some of the most innovative and promising blockchain initiatives may be tiny start-ups with small budgets that do not have fancy websites and are not getting a huge amount of public attention.

By staying informed, looking at a wide variety of projects, figuring out which problems you think could be most successfully solved by blockchain technology, and gaining exposure to alternative points of view you can develop an in-depth understanding of the blockchain space. While there are no guarantees when it comes to investing, knowing what to look for goes a long way towards helping you will make smart decisions. Blockchain is still in the early days, and making smart decisions now definitely has the potential to lead to major profits.

Limitations & Challenges of Blockchain Technology

It is one thing to understand the concept of a blockchain; it is another thing to actually build one that scales over time, remains secure, and functions in real-world scenarios. Even if you manage to accomplish all of that, the challenge of getting people to actually invest in and use your technology can prove significant. For those interested in becoming involved with blockchain space, it is worth taking some time to look at some of the potential downsides, struggles, and limitations that blockchain technology currently faces.

Speed

One of the biggest challenges facing Bitcoin, and other blockchains using a Proof-of-Work model based on Bitcoin, is speed. Because mining a block is so resource intensive and involves so much trial and error in terms of finding the proper nonce to solve a block, it takes around 10 minutes for every new block to be mined.

Not only does this utilize a massive amount of electricity, but it also means that transactions are not verified instantaneously. In fact, it can take quite awhile to see your transaction move from "pending" to "verified". As a practical matter, this makes it difficult to buy something with Bitcoin in many situations. Most people don't want to wait around at a store for an hour while their transaction goes through. Furthermore, most merchants don't want to wait to see their money come through.

Despite this issue, the number of vendors willing to accept Bitcoin is growing on a daily basis. As more implementations of blockchain technology develop, different approaches are being taken to handle the speed of transaction and verification. Ripple, for example, offers instantaneous transactions but many critics have concerns about the centralization of the underlying protocol backing the technology that makes this kind of speed possible.

As a potential investor in a new technology, it is important to ask both how this is being addressed and examine whether security is being sacrificed to maximize speed. This is certainly not always the case, but it is something to watch out for when looking into new blockchain frameworks.

Scaling

Scaling is another one of the most notable issues currently facing blockchain implementations. If you visualize the blockchain exactly as it sounds, as a long chain of blocks, you can imagine that as more transactions occur and more blocks are added the chain, the chain gets longer and longer.

Part of what makes a blockchain work is that multiple copies of it are stored and updated across a decentralized network. In theory, when a chain gets bigger, it will inevitably take up more and more space. If a chain were to get so big that it required a huge amount of storage space, those who didn't have ample room to store the chain would no longer be able to participate in the network. Thus, over time, only giant servers would suffice to store the enormous chain, leading us back the very sort of centralized model that blockchain technology was ultimately designed to avoid.

Scaling is a major problem that is being addressed in a variety of ways by innovators in the cryptocurrency and blockchain space. The "Lightning Network" is one method that has been introduced as a promising potential solution to current scaling problems faced by blockchain applications.

The Lightning Network works by allowing peer-to-peer microtransactions to happen instantaneously using blockchain smart contracts, but without adding individual transactions to the main blockchain. The Lightning Network also supports "atomic swaps" between different blockchains, i.e. from one cryptocurrency to another, so long as those chains support the same cryptographic hash functions. By combining the Bitcoin blockchain with its own, in-house, scripting language to manage smart contracts, the Lightning Network is one example of a blockchain-based solution to the problem of blockchain scaling. This is one example of how this technology builds upon itself to develop new implementations on top of the existing architecture.

Quantum computing

Quantum computers might sound like science fiction, but they are not far from becoming a reality. Without getting into the "how" of quantum computing, what we need to look at in relation to blockchain technology is the "what." What does quantum computing mean for us, generally, and what are the implications for blockchain tech?

In a nutshell, the promise of quantum computing is incredible speed and incredible power. As of now, if we look at the example of Bitcoin, we know that blocks are "mined" by a decentralized network of machines that work to verify Bitcoin transactions by solving complex math problems in exchange for a small amount of Bitcoin. When the problem is solved and the transaction is verified, a block is added to the chain.

Quantum computers would be able to solve these math problems at a rate infinitely faster than anything currently in existence. That's problem number one.

Problem number two arises when we think about the model of majority consensus that governs the Bitcoin protocol. In order to modify the blockchain, one would have to alter the record on over 50% of copies stored all around the world. Today, the kind of processing power required to do that makes hacking the blockchain effectively impossible. Quantum computing has the potential to change that, although at the moment this risk remains theoretical.

Chapter 5: The reasons why Libra will be a success

There are a couple of segments that make Libra what it is, yet the principal ones are the job of the Libra Association and the Libra save. The Libra Association is in charge of running the validator hubs, the figuring server groups that procedure exchanges, and, like this, are the main ones permitted to include or expel Libra from the course. At dispatch, the affiliation will run 100 of these hubs, yet the number will increment as scaling requires, and as more accomplices join.

This arrangement recognizes Libra from most different cryptographic forms of money. While increasingly normal cryptographic forms of money like Bitcoin are decentralized and task the person with keeping up the worldwide record by "mining" coins (for example performing cryptographically unquestionable "evidence of-work" calculations), Libra is concentrated and registered completely by the Libra validator hubs. To keep up exactness and counteract twofold spend assaults, the Libra validator hubs utilize a framework known as Byzantine adaptation to non-critical failure, in which hubs can figure out how to achieve an accord (for this situation, on the territory of Libra executed) notwithstanding when the hubs can't all concede to the condition of different hubs.

The other significant piece to Libra is its hold. Many decentralized digital currencies, remarkably Bitcoin, experience the ill effects of unstable valuation. While this can demonstrate rewarding for high-chance speculation purposes, Facebook tried to make an increasingly steady digital money to support it as a method for encouraging customary online purchaser exchanges. Libra does this by sponsoring all its issued computerized cash by a hold. Establishing Members are required to pool cash into the hold, with the possibility of arrival on their speculation utilizing profits from a low-yield venture of the save's benefits. You can likewise add to the hold when they trade fiat cash for Libra. By pegging Libra to officially sanctioned cash, the thought is that worth will remain moderately steady.

Would we be able to confide in it?

Facebook has been tormented with outrages and information ruptures over the recent years, making some legitimately questionable about the protection of this money related administrations. That being stated, Libra has some significant security that includes set up to ensure your cash.

The stage is modified in Rust, which is, for the most part, viewed as great at taking care of memory, and the keen contract component is written in Libra's very own Move language, which makes careful arrangements to limit how information can be moved. Albeit Byzantine adaptation to internal failure is viewed as the hardest class of foundational disappointments to tackle in figuring, the HotStuff convention has noteworthy qualities in its detail.

As far as protection, it is indistinct how well the stage will deal with it. Libra's site demands that "The affiliation itself isn't engaged with handling exchanges and does not store any close to home information of Libra clients," however they are in charge of running the validator hubs, which will be involved with your information. They additionally demand that they will help the law requirement, which would not be conceivable except if they held some measure of client information. Regardless of whether validator hub administrators did not share information among themselves (past what is vital for finishing client exchanges, clearly), there could be issues. On the off chance that this stage is genuinely worldwide, as Libra means, even the part of the traffic that one hub would be handle could be worthwhile for information adaptation purposes, particularly with the system beginning at just 100 hubs.

The Libra site additionally guarantees that "exchanges don't contain connections to a client's genuine personality." This likewise appears to be difficult to accept. The entire reason for how cryptographic forms of money capacity is that any spectator can check where assets have gone, a capacity which Libra has saved notwithstanding its brought together design. Regardless of whether this case is valid, personal conduct standards can undoubtedly recognize clients without unequivocal characters.

The declaration from Facebook expressed that "Calibra won't share account data or money related information with Facebook or any outsider without client assent. This implies Calibra clients' record data and budgetary information won't be utilized to improve promotion focusing on the Facebook group of items." It ought to be focused on that you actually "assent" when you consent to the arcane client understandings that accompany any application or stage, so this isn't generally a substantive confirmation from Facebook. Also, second, even though Libra may well discount advertisement deals, the information could be offered to money related organizations for use in deciding financial assessments, for example.

Considering Facebook's not exactly sterling record on client security, you are all in all correct to be suspicious of Libra's protection claims. The open-source codebase, in any case, could help lighten concerns, accepting it is appropriately reviewed by unbiased outsider onlookers and made available.

Chapter 6: Why Facebook will be the new global bank

Facebook has enlisted financial support from more than a dozen companies across the financial, e-commerce, tech and telecommunications industries to build support for the new coin project from its earliest stages. Credit card giants Visa and Mastercard, electronic payment firm PayPal Holdings and ridesharing powerhouse Uber Technologies are among the numerous businesses signed up to invest around $10 million each in Libra. The cash raised by consortium members will assist in finance the coin's launch. According to the study, in support of the new cryptocurrency initiative, Facebook has tried to increase as much as $1 billion. Libra has a leg up on other coin products as Facebook can tap into its huge, trillion-account customer base. Facebook has built between itself and Libra in layers. For example, the coin will not be controlled directly by either Facebook or the consortium's member companies, called the Libra Association, although they may help play a role in the development of the Libra payment network by acting as nodes to verify transactions.

The reason why introduced?

Internet and mobile broadband's emergence have enabled billions of individuals around the world to access global knowledge and data, high-fidelity communications, and a broad variety of more convenient, low-cost services. These services are now available from nearly anywhere in the globe using a $40 smartphone. By allowing more individuals to access the financial ecosystem, this connectivity has motivated economic empowerment. Technology firms and financial institutions have also worked together to find alternatives to boost global economic empowerment. Blockchains and cryptocurrencies have a number of unique features that could address some of the problems of accessibility and confidence. These include distributed governance (ensuring that no single entity controls the network), open access (allowing anyone with an internet connection to engage), and safety through cryptography, protecting fund integrity.

But the current blockchain schemes still need to be adopted by the mainstream. Mass-market use of current blockchains and cryptocurrencies has been hampered by their volatility and absence of scalability, which has, to date, rendered them bad value stores and exchange media. Some initiatives also directed at disrupting the current scheme and bypass regulation as opposed to innovating on compliance and regulatory fronts to enhance anti-money laundering efficiency. Working and innovating with the economic industry, including regulators and professionals across a multitude of sectors, is the only way to guarantee that this new system is supported by a viable, safe and trustworthy structure. And this approach can provide a giant leap forward towards a less expensive, more accessible, more connected global financial system.

The main objectives are to enable more individuals to access financial services, to design and manage global currency and financial infrastructure as a public good, and to promote financial inclusion, to stimulate ethical players, and to maintain the integrity of the ecosystem on an ongoing basis.

Chapter 7: How to pay with Libra

Purchasers will presumably view holding Facebook's new cash, Libra, as an option in contrast to placing cash in the bank. On the off chance that they consider it to be an appealing option, Libras could multiply. On the off chance that each Westerner held in Libra a sum equivalent to one-tenth of their bank stores today, the new money remarkable would be worth over $2trn. How stressed should banks be?

At first pass, Libra resembles a financial arrangement of sorts. The "Libra Reserve" will hold enough fluid safe resources for back each Libra it issues. A staunch minority of financial analysts has for a considerable length of time required this kind of course of action—named "limited banking"— to supplant the current "fragmentary save" model, under which stores at banks are sponsored by home loans and other illiquid advances. Thin banks, they contend, would not endure runs. Superficially, the main evident contrast between the Libra Reserve and a restricted bank is that the previous will hold resources named in an assortment of (still-to-be-indicated) monetary forms.

Facebook's digital money Libra professes to take care of an extremely critical issue: helping individuals without access to banks. I have my questions about how accommodating Libra will be.

As per the white paper, the whole purpose of Libra is to "empower basic worldwide cash and budgetary framework that enables billions of individuals." The organization claims Libra will help give individuals access to a less expensive arrangement of cash moves. Facebook refers to a measurement of 1.7 billion individuals overall who don't approach budgetary foundations, a measurement that begins with the World Bank's Global index Database 2017. Of these individuals, around 1 billion have cell phones and 500 million have web get to. Bits of knowledge like these have prompted the telephone installment framework M-Pesa, which as of now works in over 10 nations and does not utilize cryptographic money.

How about we begin with the undeniable missing measurement: we don't have the foggiest idea what number of individuals have Facebook accounts however no financial balances.

Half of all grown-ups who don't have ledgers are living in only seven nations; in four of those nations, it's difficult to perceive how Libra gets off the ground

As indicated by the report Facebook refers to, half of all grown-ups who don't have financial balances are living in only seven nations: Bangladesh, China, India, Indonesia, Mexico, Nigeria, and Pakistan. In four of these nations, it's difficult to perceive how Libra gets off the ground.

Facebook is prohibited in China. A few nations, for example, Pakistan, Indonesia, and Bangladesh have briefly restricted Facebook for timeframes, conceivably constraining the adequacy of any cash attached to the application. Facebook makes reference to this as a hazard factor to its business in its quarterly recording: "Government experts in different nations may look to confine client access to our items in the event that they believe us to be infringing upon their laws or a risk to open security or for different reasons, and sure of our items have been limited by governments in different nations now and then."

That is not every: a large number of these nations have laws around cryptographic money. (Indeed, I know it is easily proven wrong whether Libra qualifies as cryptographic money or not. Be that as it may, Facebook is considering Libra digital money, so I will expect cryptographic money laws will apply.) India's present guidelines mean Libra can't work in the nation. Pakistan is thinking about guidelines for digital forms of money, however, at present, they are prohibited. Digital currency is likewise verifiably restricted in Bangladesh and China.

The huge success here is perhaps Indonesia, which just sanctioned exchanging digital currencies, and was likewise called out by Facebook in its latest quarterly documenting as a territory of developing day by day dynamic clients.

Yet, most of these nations have generous obstacles for Libra selection. This may clarify why Libra's establishing accomplices aren't situated in any of these nations. (MercadoPago, an online installment organization that is additionally one of the accomplices, operates in Latin America and is situated in Argentina.) No establishing Libra accomplices have all the earmarks of being situated in Asia or Africa, either — and that is the place the general population without financial balances are, as indicated by the World Bank details. It isn't difficult to see something like Libra took up, however, it will need nearby help; most nations have a brush of guidelines around banking. It doesn't look like Libra has called any nearby help yet in the spots it makes a difference most.

The white paper contains some detail on Libra's engineering. In any case, there's little exchange of why individuals don't have financial balances. As indicated by the World Bank information Facebook is referring to, just about 66% of individuals who don't have financial balances state this is because they don't have enough cash to open one. Libra does not tackle that issue. 33% of individuals who don't have financial balances said they needn't bother with one. No requirement for Libra there, either.

Chapter 8: Methods on how to invest with Libra

Libra has been a work in progress for over a year on Facebook. Before distributing a white paper in mid-June, the person to person communication monster looked for and keeps on looking for, financing from organizations to help create Libra and award them access to the consortium of firms that will oversee it pushing ahead. These establishing individuals from the "Libra Association," have just been joined by significant stages like Booking.com, and Argentina-based internet business website, MercadoLibre, just as Uber, Visa, Mastercard, and PayPal. Those are some enormous players in the advanced financial world.

The declaration has some cryptographic money devotees revving their motors, making some enormous cases on Libra. The potential is positively there. Facebook's colossal impact in informing and long range interpersonal communication give it a span and straightforward entry that few organizations could want to contend with. Be that as it may, Bitcoin fans are probably not going to be as awed. Libra isn't Bitcoin, regardless of whether it shares the equivalent basic blockchain innovation and is based upon likewise open source programming. It's the nearest agent inside the current crypto-space is Ripple and its XRP token, however that brought together digital currency still isn't exactly what Libra is. Libra is progressively similar to Disney Dollars for an online environment like Facebook.

Even though not as unified as Ripple with a solitary organization controlling its future, Libra is as yet set to be overseen by a gathering of huge money related and innovative associations, just as financial speculators, telecoms, and scholarly foundations. Some of which will control the on exit ramps for a venture. That goes against the thought behind generally cryptographic forms of money.

Take Bitcoin, for instance. It's extraordinarily difficult to direct and control by its very structure. It's decentralized with nobody element ready to apply command over its blockchain, or the exchanges that happen on it. Libra is depicted as a "permission" arrange, which approves hubs and right now, requires budgetary speculation from them, to be considered.

Where Bitcoin was intended to expel the guardians from the money related world, Libra just makes Facebook and its affiliation the main watchmen that issue. Their aggregate power makes them the main ones who can mint new Libra tokens, or consume (pulverize) existing ones. With a 66% lion's share of affiliation individuals casting a ballot on it, they could even hypothetically lock individuals out of their Libra wallets, or square exchanges from occurring altogether.

With Bitcoin and most different cryptographic forms of money, none of that is conceivable. Nobody can control the cash that goes into or out of Bitcoin. That is one of its actual qualities, but at the same time is one reason it's confronted trouble with selection on a mass-showcase scale. That likely won't be an issue for Libra, yet it raises inquiries regarding the fairness of the affiliation and its individuals.

Facebook and monetary supporters like PayPal, Visa, and Mastercard will have a stake and a state in Libra's continuous advancement and however the white paper claims that the arrangement is to make Libra permissionless later on, there's no assurance of that. The investigation into it isn't planned to start for an additional five years after the dispatch one year from now, so it's very conceivable such charitable points will be unobtrusively disregarded. There's surely nothing halting new individuals from the relationship with fundamentally various thoughts regarding its activity from influencing that 66% casting a ballot lion's share later on.

Libra comprehends just the less mainstream reasons individuals don't have financial balances.

Libra comprehends just the less mainstream reasons individuals don't have financial balances. About a fourth of respondents said banks' high and unforeseen charges were in any event part of why they didn't have accounts; separation to a bank was a boundary for another 20 percent. So these individuals would appear to be Libra's intended interest group.

There's kind of an unobtrusive hitch here, however: to utilize Libra, you need to purchase Libra. I'm not the first to see it; the Financial Times' Brendan Greeley has expounded on a similar issue. The papers themselves appear to believe their end client to be somebody like me, a woman with a financial balance and a charge card. The way toward changing over to Libra is depicted practically how I would encounter it: you sign on and give them your Mastercard number or ledger number.

The issue is, individuals who don't have banks don't have financial balance numbers and they might not have charge cards, either. They have money. "There's nothing about how Libra will lower charges to change over fiat money into Libra cash, which is both the basic test of purchaser banking and an express piece of Libra's concern proclamation," Greeley composes. "Registration spots charge ghastly expenses, yet they're ready, on interest, to transform physical looks into physical money, and physical money into exchanges."

Concerning portable banking, take-up has been interwoven. M-Pesa has been fruitful in Kenya. Be that as it may, in Nigeria, individuals still lean toward money since they stress if their telephones are stolen, their cash will be gone, as well. This is an issue of social standards, not a building. Conflicts among telecoms and banks hamstrung portable financial applications in Nigeria. This, as well, isn't an issue you can unravel through the building. There are other, progressively unremarkable issues with regards to portable banking also, similar to the expense of having inert clients.

Libra doesn't address the fundamental issue the documentation says it's embarking to address

It's uncertain to me why a versatile installment administration like the one Facebook is proposing requires cryptographic money by any means. It appears like a non-starter in huge numbers of the business sectors where portable installments may be generally required. What's more, Libra doesn't address the primary issue the documentation says it's embarking to address.

From the documentation Facebook has given, a sensible individual may infer that the issue proclamation exists altogether as a smoke screen. Libra isn't intended for individuals without financial balances; it's intended for individuals who as of now have cash. Facebook is a business; organizations need to profit; as we have seen, individuals without financial balances generally don't have cash.

There's one more crimp in the documentation, which Coindesk's Ian Allison first detected: "An extra objective of the affiliation is to create and advance an open personality standard. We accept that decentralized and versatile advanced personality is essential to money related incorporation and rivalry." If Facebook's concern explanation is a trick, at that point the compact computerized character is another conceivable end game.

See, it's fine that Facebook is building a cash application for the advantaged class. That is ordinary Facebook! Yet, I don't trust Facebook is doing this for more noteworthy benefit. Perusing the documentation, it's difficult to get away from the end that all Facebook is doing is attempting to concoct another approach to line its very own pockets — regardless of whether that is Libra or an open character standard. Or on the other hand, you know, both.

Chapter 9: Some key points about Libra

Budgetary sources of Libra

The arrangement is for the Libra token to be upheld by budgetary resources, for example, a bushel of monetary standards, and US Treasury protections trying to stay away from instability. Facebook has reported that every one of the accomplices will infuse an underlying US$10 million, so Libra has full resource backing on the day it opens.

The beginning compromise of exchanges will be performed at each administration accomplice, and the blockchain's disseminated record will be utilized for a compromise between administration accomplices. The aim is to help counteract everybody except individuals from the Libra Association from attempting to remove and dissect information from the disseminated record.

Blockchain accord

Libra won't depend on digital money mining. Just individuals from the Libra Association will most likely procedure exchanges using the authorization blockchain.

Libra wants to change to a permissionless verification of-stake framework inside five years; even though their materials concede that no arrangement exists "that can convey the scale, steadiness, and security expected to help millions of individuals and exchanges over the globe through a permissionless system."

The move is the Libra blockchain's proposed keen contract and custom exchange language. It is wanted to be a statically-composed programming language, aggregated to bytecode. The venture gives this case of a Move shared exchange content in the Move white paper.

A center fundamental of Bitcoin from its initiation has been that it's decentralized. Nobody association or individual can change Bitcoin exchanges, nor would they be able to adjust wallets or square anybody from utilizing it. That is because the Bitcoin blockchain is completely decentralized, with a huge number of hubs spread everywhere throughout the world approving exchanges. There is no essential to turn into a hub, put something aside for having the PC equipment required to store the blockchain and a system association with an update it.

Those individuals can likewise run hubs in the event that they wish, however, to begin with, Facebook is relied upon to run most of them. That implies that with a straightforward vote, the individuals from the affiliation could square exchanges, change the blockchain, or even stop it briefly on the off chance that they picked up a larger part inside the Association.

That is extraordinary for blocking crime on the Libra arrange and could help return any stolen Libra to the first proprietor, yet it gives Facebook and the Association far more noteworthy controls over the digital money than anything any Bitcoin hub can have.

Programming

Libra's source code is written in Rust and distributed as open source under the Apache License with the dispatch on 18 June 2019.

Elaine Ou, a sentiment essayist at Bloomberg News, took a stab at accumulating and running the openly discharged code for Libra. As provided, the product did minimal more than enable phony coins to be placed in a wallet; practically the majority of the white paper usefulness isn't executed, including "major engineering highlights that presently can't seem to be imagined." Ou was astounded that Facebook "would discharge programming in such a state."

Guideline

Bitcoin is exceptionally difficult to direct. Organizations and governments could make the in and exit ramps for Bitcoin venture and divestment troublesome, yet as long as hubs exist someplace on the planet, Bitcoin can be executed. It could be exchanged for money, for merchandise, administrations, and all way of wares that aren't held by unified financial associations. It would be for all intents and purposes difficult to prevent

Bitcoin from being utilized completely or to try and direct it successfully.

Libra, then again, caused a tremendous blend in worldwide governments the day it was reported and its white paper uncovered. Albeit no guidelines have yet been set on it, governments are now quick to explore it and have cautioned they may direct it later on. There may likewise be endeavors at tax assessment, if conceivable.

Since Libra is a generally brought together digital money, it's superbly practical to control in these habits. While it would, in any case, be an innovative obstacle, governments can toss their weight against Facebook on the off chance that they don't care for what's going on. Not so with Bitcoin.

Advanced Wallet

Facebook plans to discharge an advanced wallet called Calibra in 2020, made accessible in Messenger, WhatsApp, just as in an independent application.

What's its value

Nobody very realizes what Libra will be worth at this time. It could be a billion dollars for each token, or a few pennies. It doesn't especially make a difference until it begins to be dispersed, yet when it becomes open, the worth ought to remain moderately consistent. Like fiat monetary forms, Libra will be sponsored by something to help keep its incentive from being excessively unpredictable. Facebook has picked a choice of true monetary standards to put together Libra's an incentive with respect to, so regardless of whether one accident, it shouldn't take Libra excessively far with it.

There has been some worry over which monetary forms will be picked, notwithstanding, and whether the expansion of new monetary forms as sponsorship, later on, could influence the cost of the tokens — bringing up issues over the monopolistic intensity of Facebook and the Libra Association.

Centralization

Bitcoin varies altogether from Facebook's new resource from multiple points of view. Maybe the most outstanding distinction lies in Bitcoin's decentralization. No single substance controls Bitcoin. Conversely, Facebook and the Libra Association have a lot of authority over the Libra resource and its utilization. The arrangement of Libra's Association likewise seems to give sizeable elements (or picked substances) control over what may turn into a top worldwide resource – the Libra. Bitcoin does not offer control to such organizations in a similar manner.

Trust and protection

As much as some may tout Bitcoin as a private, mysterious digital money, it isn't. It's semi-unknown, with no real way to demonstrate somebody possesses an unaffiliated record or wallet, yet exchanges can be followed on the open blockchain.

That is the reason those looking for additional protection and namelessness use tumblers to further muddle their actions. Altcoins like Monero offer significantly more better security for the protection seeker.

Libra, be that as it may, is obscure in this field. It's not yet certain whether exchanges can be freely followed, or whether that is something that just Facebook and the Association will approach. Facebook has expressed openly that it intends to separate church and state and keep the Facebook informal organization altogether separate from Libra, regardless of it going about as the principal stage for its utilization. In any case, with Facebook's rehashed security gaffs throughout the years and its regularly antagonistic position toward the holiness of individual information, there are worries that Facebook could use Libra buys and exchanges to advance its income from selling individual information of clients or to make notices significantly more focused on.

While Bitcoin probably won't be impeccable in its security insurances, its absence of a solitary purpose of oversight makes it far simpler to trust for some.

Facebook's Libra Asset

Working under the name Libra, Facebook's advanced resource will be utilized for worldwide installments, as per its whitepaper discharged on June 18. "Libra's main goal is to empower straightforward worldwide cash and budgetary framework that enables billions of individuals," the whitepaper states.

The whitepaper subtleties the present issues confronting worldwide funds, including constrained access for specific people and high expenses. The paper additionally calls attention to a couple of challenges, for example, the absence of reception just as instability shown by digital money resources.

In the whitepaper, the Libra has credited three key parts:

"It is based on a safe, adaptable, and solid blockchain [...] It is sponsored by a save of benefits intended to give it natural worth, and it is administered by the autonomous Libra Association entrusted with advancing the environment."

Facebook's advantage keeps running on an open-source blockchain called the Libra blockchain, and works in connection to hold, the whitepaper noted.

"Libra is completely upheld by a hold of genuine resources. A container of bank stores and momentary government protections will be held in the Libra Reserve for each Libra that is made, building trust in its inborn worth. The Libra Reserve will be directed with the target of protecting the estimation of Libra after some time."

The benefit will be a stable coin of sorts, the whitepaper expressed. "Libra is intended to be a stable advanced digital money that will be completely upheld by a save of genuine resources — the Libra Reserve — and bolstered by a focused system of trades purchasing and selling Libra." The Libra Association will be responsible for the coin supply and its connection to the hold.

As indicated by the whitepaper, "The Libra Association is an autonomous, not-revenue driven enrollment association headquartered in Geneva, Switzerland. The affiliation's motivation is to facilitate and give a system to the administration for the system and hold and lead social effect award making in the help of monetary incorporation. The affiliation's enrollment is framed from the system of validator hubs that work the Libra Blockchain."

The Libra will start as a permission blockchain, with the objective of turning into a permissionless system, the whitepaper said. Libra's blockchain additionally varies from customary blockchain innovation with respect to its chain: "The Libra Blockchain is a solitary information structure that records the historical backdrop of exchanges and states after some time."

Facebook is getting into the cryptographic money advertise. It declared a computerized wallet called Calibra on Tuesday, which it intends to dispatch in 2020.

The organization needs to be the one to bring the revealed 1.7 billion "unbanked" grown-ups into the universe of budgetary administrations under its umbrella. Be that as it may, the organization's answer isn't another Bitcoin — a long way from it. Libra, as the cash is known, is intended to permit Facebook clients to make buys on the informal organization and different sites on the web.

Chapter 10: What the Libra skeptics think

Congress ban

The U.S. representative of the House Financial Services Committee, Patrick McHenry, has written a letter to the U.S. Rep. Maxine Waters, president of the commission requesting a hearing on Project Libra.

In addition, Maxime Waters took a tough stance on Libra by calling on U.S. regulators to "wake up" and begin responding to crypto concerns about trade, cybersecurity, national security, privacy, and other concerns. She also called on Facebook to agree to a Libra project mortarium pending approval by Congress and regulators.

Carney also calls on central banks around the globe to be open-minded and to subject the project to high regulating norms because mass adopted strategies and economies are likely to be disrupted. It's understandable that the government is concerned about a global technology conglomerate that is trying to issue a digital currency that can theoretically be used better than fiat currencies issued by the government. It's almost as if in the Libra congressional hearing the US government tried to take notes from Facebook. Since 2009, however, it is only with Faceta's alleged entry into this room that the US administration was suddenly compelled to speed up the potential behind cryptocurrencies. Bitcoin and non-state-controlled currencies have been out in the open and going seriously since 2009.

It remains to be seen if Facebook could alleviate any of the concerns of the government, and given the pushback as well as the formal public responses, the schedule for Facebook's digital currency is likewise vague.

<u>Regulation</u>

Regulators are unlikely to be able to rely on international law to tackle Libra. Facebook will rely on approval in places that are strategically important to their business — especially Europe and the US. If Facebook can come out of that process with a workable solution, other governments, particularly in developing nations, may be persuaded to take a "wave it through" position that prevents extra regulatory burdens, he claims. Facebook was keen to plug Libra as a remittance solution for poor and unbanked countries.

That may mean that the Libra Association will ultimately have to contend with multi-country regulations— and that may present stumbling blocks, notes Buckley. In addition to FINMA, the Libra currency could also invite SEC regulation to consider whether Libra is a safety. In comments to the House Finance Committee on Wednesday, Gary Gensler, a former head of the

Commodity Futures Trading Commission, echoed that option, arguing that Libra resembles an exchange-traded fund, considering its multi-currency support. Some countries might decide to regulate Libra as a bank — even a systemically important bank as discussed by the US Financial Stability Oversight Council.

General skepticism around Libra

Several experts recommend caution when considering the history of mishandling user data from Facebook — as was the case with Cambridge Analytica. Now that cash is engaged, individuals are afraid that Facebook could sell banks and other interested third parties user expenditure and transactional data. After all, the company model of Facebook is to advertise by enabling scientists to access user information on a routine basis. Facebook started with a pledge to make the world more open and connected. Many believe that the only reason Facebook plans to launch the Libra coin is to "capitalize on its vast user base." Facebook will outsource Libra's management to the Libra Association Council, an independent non-profit foundation, according to the Libra white paper. The Libra blockchain is set to be an initiative of open-source blockchain offering developers a prototype in a testnet prelaunch. This will provide developers with an enhanced beta bounty program to identify system bugs, vulnerabilities, and flaws before the first half of 2020's official launch of Libra.

However, Facebook's tries to outsource Libra's management and development — by enabling anyone to create trillions of users-accessed products— placed an enormous aim on Libra that poor performers could exploit. Open-source Libra poses risks to security. These risks can potentially make it easy for a black-hat developer to create a wallet that steals funds from accounts of users. While Facebook claims to bear the cost of hacks on Calibra wallets, the Libra White Paper has not yet stipulated a system to solve such a problem in the event of significant losses. In terms of technicality, the white paper of Libra also leaves many unanswered questions, especially when it comes to the Libra blockchain's censorship resistance. Mustafa Al-Bassam, one of Chainspace's co-founders— the blockchain startup that Facebook acquired to scale Libra's research and development— points out some of the technical flaws in the Libra White Paper.

Chapter 11: Frequently asked questions about Libra

1. What is Libra network?

The Libra Blockchain is a distributed system that manages Libra ownership as well as Libra's transfer from one user to another. In the other words, every Libra user needs to see a consistent view of the system— otherwise criminal might be able to trick someone into thinking they have been paid, although payment has never been made. This is referred to as a "double assault on expenditure."

2. Kindly explain the Libra Brand?

While it is far too early for anyone to have a truly informed handle on what many expect to be the next titanium of cryptocurrency, it cannot be asserted that this is anything but an important milestone for digital currency proponents.

Whether Libra is truly decentralized or even crypto at all, many might contend, but the ramifications of how this will play out as a native token of the world's biggest digital ecosystem have many hypothesizing what this implies for Facebook and other social media platforms ' incentive systems.

This may lead to better protection of Facebook's user data, rather than further marketing of behavioral metrics, as

Facebook will be encouraged to guarantee that its customers continue to purchase and sell Libra, and protecting its users' metadata will be critical to gaining confidence.

The feedback loop between the customer and the network will be much quicker by adding a financial layer. If the network does not take care of those who use the currency's interests, consumers will stop using the currency. The currency can assist maintain the network responsibly and aligned with its customers in this manner.

Another possible result is that Facebook will be able to discern true accounts from fake accounts (or trolls) that presently populate news feeds from Facebook and assist propagate fake news.

Facebook could recognize botnets based on trade history and then position it at a reduced priority for real customers — weighted "crowd wisdom" assessment if you like.

3. What do you understand with the Libra audience?

Libra's primary audience is 1.7 billion adults worldwide without access to a traditional bank, though 1 billion have a mobile phone and almost half a billion have access to the internet. It will allow them to send and receive money through their phones. These transactions will be made cheaper by Libra than other non-bank alternatives. Users will be able to make purchases online with no credit card, and the lowest fee possible. It also is going to be a convenient way to transfer money from one side of the globe to another.

Facebook seems to pin its hopes on the libra coin to solve this problem as it will ensure that digital banking services reach unbanked parts of the world. Countries like India desperately need such service primarily in terms of remittances— with almost 200 million individuals using WhatsApp. The country's diaspora remittance market is one of the largest in the world, with the World Bank estimating that in 2018 alone, approximately 80 million dollars were remitted to the country.

4. What is Libra stability?

The goal is to make Libra more useful than any other national currency, accepted in more places and with fewer complications; it would only be held back by attaching it to a single national currency.

However, unlike most stable coins, Libra is not attached to a particular currency. While a Libra Reserve exists, Libra does not appear to be necessarily attached to its value. Instead, the reserve works as a kind of lower bound to the value of Libra. That implies there's only one Libra, regardless of where you live.

5. What is Libra simplicity?

It should be easy and intuitive to secure your economic resources on your mobile device. Globally moving cash should be as simple and cost-effective as sending a text message or sharing a picture, regardless of where you live, what you do, or how much you gain.

A simple global currency means "supermoney," higher than the dollar, the euro, or any government-owned currency. A financial infrastructure means we can send that money around the world, quickly and cheaply.

Libras concept is pretty simple. You're depositing real money and getting almost the same amount of Libra coins back or buying it from the Wallet app. Importantly, you can do whatever you like, starting with buying stuff on eBay and ending with paying for your Uber. Moreover, you will have easy access to it since every app that Facebook possesses, Calibra, wallet for the Libra coin, is going to be: WhatsApp, Messenger, Facebook, or Calibra itself, meaning that anyone with a smartphone can get their hands on the Libra coin.

Conclusions

It is too early right now to say anything decisive for Libra because it has just been announced yet and has about a year to show up in the market is all goes according to the plan. However, once it appears In the market there will still be a lot of challenges which it will have to face to stay relevant such as the big financial institutions like the banks and the government which will try their utmost to limit this currency and impose sanctions on it just like they did for Bitcoin and then comes acceptability that whether the people trust facebook for their monetary transactions and with the security and safety of their money. On the other hand if Libra manages to tackle all of these issues then it can emerge as a Global economy in the World and may play a huge part in shaping and driving the Economy of the World. But still it is too early to come to a final conclusion as this currency is yet to be released and once it hits the market and spends some time there only then we will be able to draw a clear picture of what this currency's impact will be on the World and its Economy.

As for all the kinds of advancements in Bitcoins and Altcoins we have examined all through the book, it will require the responsibility and coordinated effort of governments, innovation firms, and scholarly organizations. This joint effort could prompt supportable monetary development and the advancement of our general society. We are at a crucial point in our history where through advances in technology we have been given both the blessing and the obligation of huge sums of information and the apparatuses to translate and make new boondocks in numerous fields.

Digital money is a standout among the most talked about advances. Innovation has empowered access to make and exchange advanced money and put the chance to take an interest under the control of the general population in a decentralized and not completely regulated way. At its center, government has the obligation to secure its natives, to provide parameters for conduct, and to accommodate their prosperity. In that vein, it is government that records and stores the recordation life's most fundamental and major occasions and events.

Right when a child is born, it is government that gives the birth confirmation. Exactly when that identical tyke transforms into an adult and purchase a home, purchase a vehicle, cast a ticket in choices, and possibly gets hitched, it is government that records and stores that data. Finally, when that proportional individual passes away, it is government that issues a passing verification.

www.ingramcontent.com/pod-product-compliance
Lightning Source LLC
Chambersburg PA
CBHW070644220526
45466CB00001B/286